Interpretationshilfen

Brave New World

Aldous Huxley

Cornelsen

Bernhard J. Müller
Brave New World · Interpretationshilfe

Verlagsredaktion
Neil Porter

Umschlagdesign
Klein & Halm Grafikdesign, Berlin

Technische Umsetzung
Antje Kanniga, Köln

Bilder: S. 5: © ullstein bild – ullstein bild; S. 87: © Christian Darkin / Alamy; S. 88: © NoRB_photography /Alamy; S. 91: picture-alliance/maxppp/Costa/ Leemage; S. 95: Mary Evans Picture Library; S. 97 (links): © picture-alliance / KPA / TopFoto; S. 97 (rechts): © Rykoff Collection / Corbis; S. 99: Reprinted courtesy of HowStuffWorks.com.

www.cornelsen.de

1. Auflage, 1. Druck 2008

Druck: CS-Druck CornelsenStürtz, Berlin

ISBN 978-3-589-04536-5

Inhalt gedruckt auf säurefreiem Papier aus nachhaltiger Forstwirtschaft.

Contents

All page and line references are to the Cornelsen edition of *Brave New World* (Berlin: Cornelsen Verlag, 2007); ISBN 978-3-06-031163-7.

Aldous Huxley

Aldous L. Huxley (1894–1963) was born into an upper-middle-class family in Godalming, Surrey, a small town not far from London. Notable ancestors included his grandfather Thomas H. Huxley, a famous scientist who helped develop Charles Darwin's evolution theory, and his great-uncle Matthew Arnold, a celebrated poet. Huxley received an excellent education at Eton College and then at Balliol College, Oxford. He had hoped to become a doctor, but a serious eye disease almost blinded him at the age of 16. In 1915 he graduated from Oxford University with a degree in English Literature and became a journalist, covering a wide range of topics and literary genres.

After writing essays, short stories and poetry, Huxley published his first novel *Crome Yellow* in 1921, which laid the foundation for his reputation as a witty and sometimes cynical novelist. Other successful novels followed before his masterpiece *Brave New World* was published in 1932. Although the author himself did not consider the novel his best, it is the book for which he is most remembered. Huxley conceived the idea of writing his satire about the decay of society after a trip to the United States in 1925 and 1926, during which his cultural pessimism was intensified by his realization of how technological and economic progress was accompanied by the growth of an influential mass media.

Following the devastation of World War II and the use of the first atomic bombs, Huxley added a foreword in 1946 commenting on the novel and recent events and developments.

In *Brave New World* many strands of Huxley's life came together. Firstly, he was able to make use of his extraordinary critical intellect and his excellent education. He had also inherited from his father and grandfather, both of whom were biologists, a fascination for contemporary scientific developments. Coming as he did from a wealthy, intellectual family, he felt a certain contempt for the masses, mass production and mass entertainment. And finally, the depressing experience of the slaughter of World War I, with its aftermath of totalitarian regimes offering supposedly perfect solutions for the problems of society, encouraged in Huxley a sceptical view of future history that seemed to offer only a choice between dictatorship and destruction. Before he wrote *Brave New World*, Huxley had already touched on loveless sex, the decay of culture and scientific progress in earlier novels like *Antic Hay* (1923) and *Point Counter Point* (1928).

In 1938, at the zenith of his career, Huxley moved to California. He continued writing, and became more and more involved with mysticism. He also became interested in the effects of hallucinogenic drugs; his experiences here are described in *The Doors of Perception* (1954). It was only in his last novel *Island* (1962) that Huxley returned to the subject of a utopian society, but offered in this novel a more optimistic vision of a future society.

While Huxley left behind an enormous large body of work, his books – though popular in his time – are today largely forgotten, with the exception of *Brave New World*. This may be due to the fact that his novels are driven by ideas and are, as a consequence, intellectually demanding; and that the plots and characters, being secondary to the intellectual agenda of the books, are not immediately 'gripping' and so do not grab the readers' attention and imagination in a quick and easy manner.

Synopsis

The novel is set in the year 2540. The world consists of one state that has organized the lives of human beings so that nobody can be unhappy.

Most of the action is set in London. At the beginning of the novel the process of cloning and conditioning is being explained to some students, which gives the reader an introduction to the fundamentals of this utopia, based as it is on producing happy individuals for each of the five levels of society, ranging from the intelligent Alphas to the simple Epsilons.

The novel does not have a protagonist, but centres instead around a group of Alphas and Betas. Bernard Marx has a misshapen body and seems to be ill at ease with the rules of society; Helmhotz Watson is a good-looking and successful man who feels that something is missing in his life; Lenina Crowne is a pretty young woman who also does not strictly adhere to the rules of society, as she has a tendency to have affairs which last longer than is usual in a system that disapproves of intense personal and love relations.

Lenina is intrigued by Bernard Marx, who refuses to have sexual affairs, which may also be due to his strange looks and sense of his own inferiority. Lenina cannot understand why he wants to be alone with her together and not immediately have sex, as she enjoys sex. Due to his anti-social behaviour, Bernard is often looked down upon by others. His boss has decided that he is an unsettling factor at work and wants to have him exiled to Iceland.

Bernard and Lenina spend a holiday together in a Reservation in New Mexico, where the inhabitants live like 'savages', worshipping ancient gods who they appease by performing rites of atonement and purification. Here they meet John, whose mother is from the civilized world and was abandoned there by Bernard's boss following an accident. John's mother never managed to feel at home in the Reservation, while John has been made to feel like an alien there due to his non-Indian blood and his mother's 'immoral behaviour'. John is an admirer of Shakespeare, whose words he uses to express his own feelings.

Bernard and Lenina take John and his mother back to London. While John wants to have a love relationship with Lenina, Lenina wants to have sex with him. Bernard, on the other hand, wants to use John for social advancement. Bernard manages to get his boss removed after it is revealed that he is the natural father of John – being a father is a taboo in this family-less world. Bernard then uses John to be introduced to all the important people in society. Once Bernard has become a minor celebrity, women want to have sex with him, which Bernard suddenly seems to enjoy.

As John becomes disillusioned with the new society in which he finds himself, he refuses to allow Bernard to use him for his own purposes and Bernard falls from grace, becoming miserable again. Lenina and John never manage to work out what they want from each other. Ultimately John is unable to integrate into the utopian society, as it lacks the depth and emotion he requires. Following a mini-riot which John tries to provoke with Helmholtz's help, Bernard and Helmholtz are exiled. John decides to live as a hermit in the country. But he is pestered by journalists, and when a crowd of onlookers gathers to watch him and ends up having a mass orgy in which he participates, John commits suicide.

The Story

Chapter One

Summary: The novel begins in the Central London Hatchery and Conditioning Centre in the year A.F. 632. The Director of Hatcheries and Conditioning (the D.H.C) is guiding a group of new students around his institution, introducing them to the principles of the mass production of human beings.

A tour of the Hatchery

The guided tour starts in the Fertilizing Room, where ova are fertilized artificially in vitro. The treatment with X-rays and alcohol, called Bokanovsky's Process, produces up to 96 identical twins from one egg.

Human eggs are fertilized and then manipulated.

In the Bottling Room the fertilized eggs are transferred from test-tubes to bottle-like containers, in which they develop under conditions regulated according to the needs of society. Moving on through the Centre, the group of students meets Lenina, who is busy inoculating the embryos against various diseases.

On an assembly-line in the Social Predestination Room, the embryos undergo a process that adapts them perfectly to their future role in society. The addition or reduction of oxygen determines the intelligence of the embryos according to the requirements of their future class.

Commentary: The function of the first three chapters is to introduce the reader to the World State. The setting of the novel is London in the year A.F. 632, although the meaning of 'A.F.' and its implications are not explained yet.

A.F. = After Ford

In the first paragraph Huxley presents the state's motto – COMMUNITY, IDENTITY, STABILITY – which lists the ideals of the World State. The description of the Hatchery creates an atmosphere of a cold, technocratic and artificial world. This impression is enhanced by the D.H.C.'s explanation of the mass production of human beings. The production process aims for stability by supplying society with the members that it needs, and by conditioning people to be satisfied with, and even enjoy, the role they are given by the state.

The Director is a pedantic man.

There are 5 different castes.

The D.H.C. is enthusiastic about the achievements of science in the service of a totalitarian society, and the students unquestioningly accept what the Director says. The reader may be shocked to learn that people are no longer regarded as individuals, but as cogs in the state machine.

Huxley extrapolates contemporary ideas into possible future applications: the possibilities of mass production (*'at last applied to biology'*, p.9, ll.13–14), the problem of overpopulation, progress in genetic engineering (the foundations of which were researched in the 1920s), and discoveries in the field of learning (the process of conditioning).

Note that the main characters are not introduced in the first chapter.

The reader has not yet been introduced to any characters who make an impression. When the first characters do make an appearance, the reader already knows how they have been created and formed. At the end of the chapter the brief encounter between Henry Foster and Lenina Crowne, two employees at the Hatchery, makes the reader curious about what personal relationships are like in such a world.

Chapter Two

Summary: The Director's tour continues in the Infant Nurseries – Neo-Pavlovian Conditioning Rooms. Here the group witnesses an example of conditioning: low-caste babies are offered flowers and books, which they, full of curiosity, try to reach. At the Director's signal terrifying sirens shriek and the infants are given slight electric shocks. When the books and flowers are presented again, the children shrink from them in horror because they have learned to associate them with negative experiences. The reason for this process is that the lower castes are not supposed to read books, which are considered a waste of time and might foster non-conformist ideas, while the love of flowers is useless as it does not encourage consumption. People are conditioned to enjoy leisure activities requiring a lot of equipment, which keeps production going.

Conditioning is used to encourage the children to like and dislike things.

Afterwards the Director explains the principles of hypnopaedia, or sleep-teaching. He talks about the past when human beings still had parents (a taboo word in the World State). Psychologists have discovered that sleep-teaching is not a suitable method of learning facts, but is ideal for moral education. Hence, during their sleep young children listen to tapes that permanently repeat slogans about desirable and undesirable behaviour and attitudes, which then remain engraved in their minds for the rest of their lives. The students are shown an example of Elementary Class Consciousness, in which Beta children are taught to be happy to belong to their own caste.

Hypnopaedia is used for moral education.

Commentary: While the first chapter concentrates on the biological formation of the individual human being, the second chapter shows how the manipulation of individuals is continued after birth (or decanting, as it is called in the novel). With the help of extremely negative experiences unwanted behaviour is erased. The learning theory of conditioning goes back to the Russian psychologist Ivan Pavlov (cf. p. 99), who experimented with dogs, and his American colleague Watson, who applied Pavlov's findings to human beings. The World State has perfected their crude psychological theories. The aim of all conditioning is to make *'people like their unescapable social destiny'* (p. 16, l. 27), as personal satisfaction with one's individual life is the foundation of the stability of society.

While conditioning can only be used for basic instincts, sleep-teaching is far more subtle. It is employed to instil moral values and judgements in the children's minds. As with conditioning, the scientists of the future have perfected a learning process that was discovered in Huxley's lifetime.

Conditioning and sleep-teaching serve to strengthen two basic elements of society: the caste system and the need for consumption. The adherence to a special caste is predestined before birth and is cemented by an education that reinforces the traits of a particular caste. At the end of the educational process each person has learned to like their caste and their caste only, which is the World State's recipe for satisfaction and, hence, stability.

People are taught to be happy with their social caste..

The pattern of permanent consumption is stamped into the young brains as well. For the state, consumption means that production continues, ensuring prosperity and gainful employment. For the individual there is always some form distraction and therefore no reason to

Consumption is important as it makes the state viable.

question anything. Thus consumption contributes to the stability of the state.

The Director speaks derisively about living conditions at the beginning of the 20th century, especially the natural method of reproduction and traditional family life, which are looked upon with horror now. Huxley wants the reader to see the difference between both worlds clearly, which is a typical trait of a novel of ideas.

Living conditions in the 20th century are satirized.

With the same ironic undertone Huxley presents the World State's surrogate of the Christian religion. Henry Ford is equated with Jesus as the hero of a new cult of mass culture, and time is measured from the invention of Ford's Model T, the first car ever produced on an assembly line.

For more information on Henry Ford cf. p. 97.

Chapter Three

Summary: Outside in the garden the group observes children playing erotic games. A boy who does not want to take part is taken to a psychologist to check if he is abnormal. The D.H.C. tells the students about the suppression of erotic games in the past, which seems incredible to them.

Children are encouraged to play sexual games.

Suddenly one of the ten rulers of the World State, World Controller Mustapha Mond, appears, and gives a lecture on history. He explains that *'history is bunk'* (i.e. nonsense – a quotation from Henry Ford) and describes the intolerable living conditions of former family life, which was based on strong emotions and feelings of exclusivity, which only led to trouble and instability. To achieve the prime goal of stability, the old world with its emotions, religion and political ideas such as democracy and liberalism was overthrown, and

One of the World Controllers explains why it was necessary to change society.

the mechanisms of the new society were established.

The turning point was the Nine Years' War in A.F. 141, which brought about great devastation and left people with a choice between the destruction of humankind and the erection of the World State. As a consequence, the artificial production of human beings, conditioning, and hypnopaedia were introduced. Books, monuments and all memories of the past were eradicated, Ford's introduction of the T-Model car was chosen as the opening date of the new era. A perfect drug called *soma* was invented to satisfy all the needs society could not fulfil. Finally, even old age was conquered.

The destruction that humanity brought upon itself led to the formation of a new society.

Intertwined with Mond's account are three other strands: while getting ready for her evening appointment with Henry Foster, Lenina and her friend Fanny talk about their sex life and Lenina's interest in Bernard Marx, who is said to be a little strange due to a mistake in his production. In another strand, Marx himself overhears Foster chatting with a friend about Lenina; he strongly dislikes the way they talk about women as if they were meat. A third strand consists of hypnopaedic fragments.

Commentary: The introduction to the World State is completed by a look at sexual education, which explains why people behave as they do in the novel, and at the historical developments that led to this near-perfect state. According to Mond, history is 'bunk' because the study of history always describes developments and as the new order no longer allows any major changes, history has become irrelevant. Moreover, historical studies would allow for informed comparisons between the contemporary world and former

Freud's ideas concerning sexual repression are satirized here, as children are now *forced* to play sexual games.

conditions, which is not desired by the rulers of the World State.

Huxley introduces the character of Mustapha Mond as one of the rulers (Controllers) of the state. As someone with deep insight into what is going on, Mond provides further background information on the World State that, on the one hand, is amusing because of his ironic presentation of the past, but also necessary for a better understanding of the action.

Mond's contempt for the past is supposed to provoke readers into an awareness of their own values: real happiness is a transient reward in a world that knows strong emotions and suffering, whereas in this State real happiness has been replaced by the immediate satisfaction of all desires, particularly sexual.

Through an impressionistic montage of fragments from different conversations and situations, Huxley contrasts different views of personal relationships: the old kind of family life and romance, Bernard's critical view of promiscuity, the girls' discussion about various aspects of their sex lives, and the men's small talk about Lenina's sexual qualities. The same technique is used to comment indirectly on consumption, *soma* and religion.

As soon as we are introduced to some characters, we see through their words and thoughts that the system is not perfect.

With Chapter Three the description of the society ends, and the conversations dealing with Lenina and Bernard prepare the way for the start of the real plot in the next chapter.

Chapter Four

Summary: (Part 1) Lenina meets Bernard in a crowded lift and asks him openly about their plan to go to the Savage Reservation in New Mexico,

Lenina and Bernard talk about their plan to visit the Reservation.

which embarrasses him. Then she goes off to play Obstacle Golf with Henry Foster.

(Part 2) Bernard is uncertain about Lenina, since on the one hand she wants to go on holiday with him, but on the other hand she spends the evening with Henry. Owing to his physical defects Bernard feels insecure and inferior with women or lower castes. Bernard picks up Helmholtz Watson, a handsome and highly intelligent Emotional Engineer, by plane, and they fly home. Both feel like individuals, and consequently like outsiders. But whereas Bernard boasts of his date with Lenina, Helmholtz has become tired of his success with women and his many leisure activities, and is searching for something more fulfilling.

We learn about Bernard's and Helmholtz's dissatisfaction with the system.

Commentary: Lenina is a typical product of the World State. Speaking to Bernard about their holiday in public shows that she feels no need to treat her personal relationships as a private matter. Bernard, however, lacks the ease of other people, especially as far as sex is concerned. Due to his diminutive size (allegedly because of a mistake during his production) he suffers from an inferiority complex, which makes him insecure when dealing with women or lower castes, who have difficulty recognizing him as an Alpha as they have been conditioned to respond to the size of other people. Bernard is dissatisfied with the world because his low self-confidence prevents him from enjoying the opportunities of society.

Not having the right appearance makes Bernard feel he is not part of society.

The feeling of being an outcast connects Bernard with Helmholtz. In every respect Helmholtz is the perfect Alpha-Plus, maybe even '*a little* too *able*' (p. 58, ll. 15–16) in the eyes of his superiors. Despite being very successful, Helmholtz has recently begun to feel that there

Being too perfect makes Helmholtz feel like an outsider.

must be more to life – though he does not really know what that might be.

Chapter Four, in which the actual plot starts, contrasts an evening spent by Henry and Lenina, who are able to enjoy themselves as well-adapted members of society, and by the outsiders Bernard and Helmholtz, who cannot get satisfaction from ordinary, shallow pleasures. Huxley depicts both pairs flying over London, and uses these flights to show the changes London and its suburbs have undergone in this new world – mostly by increasing the areas given over to public amusements and sports.

Chapter Five

Summary: (Part 1) On their way back from Obstacle Golf, Henry and Lenina fly over the Slough Crematorium where corpses are burnt to recover phosphorus, which is used as a fertilizer. They discuss the chemical equality of all people, and what it must be like to be an Epsilon. They come to the conclusion that everybody is happy, which makes them pleased with society as they know it. After dinner they go to a club, and their perfect evening ends up with the couple having sex in Henry's apartment.

Even after death people are useful for society.

An evening out consists of sport, dancing, soma and sex.

(Part 2) Bernard takes part in a Solidarity Service with eleven other people. The participants take *soma* and sing hymns, waiting for the coming of the 'Greater Being', the climax of the event. Once the participants have reached a state of ecstasy, the service finishes in a sex orgy. But whereas everybody else enjoys the feeling of unity, Bernard feels more isolated than ever.

Solidarity Services fulfil the needs of a religious service.

Commentary: The discrepancy between Lenina's and Henry's happiness and Bernard's loneliness intensifies in this chapter. The first two enjoy the entertainment facilities: a variety of sports, the latest synthetic music, a scent and colour organ which appeals to every sense, dancing with hundreds of people, sex and *soma*. What is more, they also love the existing social order, in which everyone has their function, and everyone serves society even after death through phosphorus recovery. Huxley ironically reduces the equality of all men – the foundation of modern democracy and human rights – to a physico-chemical equality.

It is interesting to note how similar entertainment in our world is to entertainment in the World State.

The contentment of Lenina and Henry is sharply contrasted with Bernard's inability to conform. Huxley, who was critical of organized religion and who favoured mysticism, portrays the Solidarity Service as a satire of a Christian service. Traditional Christian elements are altered in an absurd way: the cross becomes a T, communion becomes a sex and *soma* party, the community in God becomes an orgy, while the hymns have ridiculous, infantile texts (e.g. 'Orgy-porgy'), etc.

Throughout the novel there is an underlying criticism of religion.

Chapter Six

Summary: (Part 1) Lenina ponders upon her relationship with Bernard. She finds him quite 'odd', but on the other hand, as an Alpha-Plus psychologist, he offers her the rare chance to visit the Reservation. What disturbs Lenina most is Bernard's mania for doing things in private. While she wants to do sports, he prefers walking and talking alone with her. He refuses to take *soma* when he is in a bad mood. On their flight back from the Women's Heavyweight Wrestling Championships in Amsterdam, Bernard turns off

Lenina and Bernard have different ideas of what happiness is.

the helicopter engines to look at the sea, the moon and the stars in peace, but Lenina is bored and even horrified by the silence and the night-time seascape. Bernard philosophizes about not wanting to be '*just a cell in the social body*' and '*enslaved by my conditioning*' (p.78, ll.8, 21); he wants to be happy in his own individual way. Lenina, however, replies with sleep-teaching slogans and considers his thinking dangerous for society. Realizing that she cannot understand him, he gives in, takes *soma*, and has sex with her. The next day he tries to make it clear to Lenina that he would have preferred to have waited and let their relationship grow before having sex, because he wants '*to know what passion is*' and '*to try the effect of arresting my impulses*' (p.80, ll.28, 21–22). Despite their differences, Lenina is still interested in him.

(Part 2) Bernard goes to the D.H.C. to have his permit to enter the Reservation authorized. The Director recounts his own experiences in the Reservation some 20 years before. He had been accompanied by a Beta-Minus who suddenly disappeared and was never found again. After telling Bernard his story he feels embarrassed at having given away something personal. He threatens to banish Bernard to Iceland if there are any more reports about his abnormal behaviour.

Bernard gets his permit to visit the Reservation and learns about the D.H.C.'s trip there many years ago.

In the evening Bernard narrates the incident to Helmholtz and pretends to have reacted boldly to the threat of exile. Helmholtz does not like Bernard's boasting and self-pity, but Bernard is the only one he can talk to about the things that move him.

(Part 3) Bernard and Lenina travel to the Reservation and stay at Santa Fé for the night. The next day a warden provides them with information on the size of the Reservation and its

Bernard and Lenina fly to the Reservation.

inhabitants. An electric fence prevents the 'savages' from escaping – past attempts to break free were put down with gas bombs. The savages have preserved their traditional way of living; they still marry and have children, they still practise religion, and they speak languages that are extinct elsewhere.

Since Bernard is afraid he has left an expensive eau de cologne tap running in his bathroom in London, he calls Helmholtz to take care of it and hears from him that the D.H.C. has decided to send Bernard to Iceland. Whereas in the past Bernard felt elated by the Director's threats, imagining in them a chance to prove his heroism, he is now shocked, and ends up taking *soma*.

Bernard learns that he will be exiled.

Later, a plane takes the couple to their hotel at Malpais in the Reservation.

Commentary: The relationship between Bernard and Lenina is growing closer, although it is difficult to understand what attracts them to each other. Lenina, a typical product of the World State, is only interested in superficial entertainment, *soma*, and sex, and only thinks in terms of hypnopaedic slogans. She is fascinated by the fact that Bernard is different, yet whenever he talks about being different or behaving in a way that is unorthodox, she is repelled. Bernard is proud of having a date with such an attractive woman, but he also despises her for her conformism.

Bernard seeks solitude as it gives him time to reflect on himself; Lenina (like a good citizen) fears being alone.

So their expectations when they fly to the Reservation are very different: Lenina is looking forward to a thrilling adventure, Bernard wants to be alone with her, far from so-called civilization. Their holidays are overshadowed by the Director's threat to ban Bernard to Iceland for inappropriate behaviour. Yet from what the D.H.C. had told

Bernard, the reader knows that he has an embarrassing secret connected with the Reservation.

Bernard is portrayed as an inconsistent character: he spends the holidays with someone who cannot understand him; he boasts about his courage, but is in reality a self-pitying coward; he is waiting for a challenge, but fails to live up to it.

To some extent the Savage Reservation resembles a human zoo or prison, where the squalid and primitive conditions contrast with the comfortable lifestyle in the rest of the world.

The Warden's delivery of information reminds one of the Director's in Chapter One.

Chapter Seven

Summary: A guide leads Bernard and Lenina from the hotel to the pueblo of Malpais. Lenina is ill at ease due to the guide, who is unfriendly and smelly, and due to the fact that she has to walk in the heat. On entering the village she is disgusted by the dirt, a decrepit old man, and women who are breast-feeding. Bernard's attempts to explain the different world to her fail. Without the comfort of *soma*, the horrors of Malpais make her wish she had never come.

Life in the Reservation is a total contrast to that in the World State.

On a wide terrace, the two tourists are witness to an indigenous ceremony: a young man is whipped in a ritual dance until he collapses. When Linda turns away in utter disgust, an Indian with a European complexion appears and greets them in peculiar English (that will later turn out to be Shakespearean). He tells the visitors that he himself wanted to be the sacrifice in the fertility rite in order to prove his courage and endurance, but was refused by the community. He reveals that he is John, the son of the D.H.C. and the girl who vanished after an accident in the Reservation

Some form of religious celebration takes place.

John introduces himself to Bernard and Lenina.

some 20 years before. From the very first moment, John is enchanted by Lenina, the most beautiful woman he has ever seen.

When John brings the guests to his mother Linda's house, Lenina is shocked by the squalor and the woman's revolting appearance. Seeing Lenina reminds Linda of her past, the luxury in 'the Other Place' (the World State), and of her misery as an outsider in the Indian world. As a Beta she had enormous difficulties getting used to the dirt and the cheap alcohol, while her conditioning in the Other World taught her to be promiscuous, which caused the Indians to treat her as a whore.

John's mother is a sad wreck of human being.

Commentary: In this chapter the reader learns about the Reservation. The overall impressions of filth, illness, and poverty, and the brutality of the fertility rite present a sharp contrast to the uniform pleasures of the civilized world and its pseudo-religious Solidarity services. The reader is offered an alternative to the cold, emotionless futuristic society, but this primitive alternative seems no better. People live in squalor and misery and adhere to superstitions.

Linda reveals that the Reservation is just as cruel a place as the World State, as she poses a threat to the Reservation's notions of community, identity and stability.

Due to her conditioning, Lenina is incapable of the slightest understanding whatsoever for the Indians' way of life. Her initial attempts to compare elements of the Reservation to London soon give way to a complete rejection of the primitive lifestyle and superstition of the natives. She regrets having come to this place for a holiday.

Bernard, on the other hand, tries to find positive aspects: he wonders whether the intimate relationships within families and the independence from an all-powerful state might not be desirable. He offers Lenina explanations for what they see, partly to make Lenina understand the Indians, as her failure to do so could jeopardize the success of their holiday, but partly to demonstrate his unorthodoxy. Of course, his sympathetic attitude towards an alternative life does not mean that he likes all its aspects.

With John, the savage, a new character is introduced who will have a major impact on the further course of the novel. John is an outsider in the Reservation and is keen to discuss life in both the Reservation and the outside world with Bernard. Now that he is certain that John is the D.H.C.'s son, Bernard feels he has a stronger hand in dealing with his superior when it comes to his banishment to Iceland.

John will become one of the major characters in the novel.

Never having seen a beautiful woman like Lenina before, John immediately feels attracted to her. Later (in Chapter Eleven) their relationship becomes quite close, with John replacing Bernard as Lenina's admirer, but he too will not find in her what he is looking for.

Linda serves as an example of how people from the civilized world have been made incapable of coping with circumstances other than those for which they have been conditioned. Her life in the Reservation is a failure, as she is unable to adapt. In the absence of *soma* and other facilities that make life easier, she succumbs to alcohol, while her need to consume and live promiscuously have no place a world in which traditional values like thrift and monogamy still predominate.

Chapter Eight

Summary: In a conversation with Bernard, John recounts some of his childhood memories. He remembers his mother being visited by Popé, her lover, and various other men. Once, three Indian women whipped Linda because she had slept with their husbands. Linda often drowned her misery in alcohol. She talked to him about the 'The Other Place', which has a mythical status in John's imagination.

The reader learns of John's childhood (this is unusual, as none of the other character's childhoods are mentioned).

Linda taught John to read and write, first with the help of a manual for Embryo-Store workers, which she had accidentally brought with her to the Reservation, and later with Shakespeare's *Complete Works*, which Popé had found somewhere. John was fascinated by Shakespeare's language and was astonished to find his own feelings expressed in his writing. The reading of *Hamlet* encouraged him to attempt to try to kill Popé, who he hated for the way he treated his mother.

As an adolescent John learned the myths of the Indians. When he first fell in love, he had to accept that the girl he was in love with married someone else and so, according to local traditions, was lost to him forever. His violent exclusion from an initiation rite drove him into the loneliness of the mountains, where he was tempted to commit suicide, but he refrained from doing so, which led him to encounter for the first time the concepts of time, death and God. Excluded from the initiation rites of the other youths, he tried to find his own way by fasting and self-punishment, such as standing in the heat of the sun like the crucified Jesus till he fainted.

Both Bernard and John try to find themselves in solitude.

Planning to put pressure on the D.H.C., but also feeling a bond with John as an outsider in his society, Bernard invites him and his mother to London. Believing that his dreams are finally going to come true, John repeatedly quotes from Shakespeare's play *The Tempest: 'O brave new*

Bernard plans to take John back to London.

world!' He is even more delighted when he discovers that Bernard is not married to Lenina.

Commentary: This chapter reveals John's upbringing in the reservation. His position as a social outcast has given him deep and painful insights into life, while his knowledge of the works of Shakespeare help him express and understand much of what he has gone through. He encounters and overcomes extreme situations with courage. As such, he is the only character in the novel with sufficient self-knowledge to be able to look critically at the modern world. Yet his insistence on physical pain as a means of strengthening his character is typical of someone with a Reservation upbringing. His experiment in re-living Jesus's crucifixion foreshadows John's death at the end of the novel. John has achieved in practice what Bernard is striving for theoretically – to be a critical outsider.

John enthusiastically accepts Bernard's invitation to go to London, expecting some kind of paradise in the civilized world. John's elation finds expression in the line '*O brave* (i.e beautiful) *new world*' from Shakespeare's *The Tempest*, in which a young woman after a long time alone on an island meets other people for the first time. John's naïve anticipation is an example of dramatic irony, as the reader already knows what sort of civilization really awaits him.

The first use of the phrase 'brave new world'.

Chapter Nine

Summary: Bernard obtains permission from World Controller Mond to take John and Linda to London. In the meantime Lenina has taken lots of *soma* to relax after the experiences in the Reservation. Because she asked John to meet her,

John comes to her apartment, only to find her in a drugged sleep. Full of awe and desire, John first searches her personal belongings, then stands next to her sleeping body, torn between the temptation to touch her and the chivalrous ideal of self-control. Shakepeare lends him the words to express his feelings. On hearing Bernard return, John escapes in panic.

John has strong feelings for Lenina.

Commentary: Now that Bernard has been given permission to bring Linda and John to the civilized world, the reader expects confrontations between John and the modern world on the one hand, and between John and Bernard as rivals for Lenina's love on the other hand.

The use of inappropriate words from Shakespeare to idealize Lenina is an indication that despite (or rather because of) his desire for her, John seems intent on viewing Lenina not as she is, but as someone who conforms to the ideals expressed by Shakespeare.

Whereas John refuses to act on his sexual desires, Lenina would almost certainly have done so.

Chapter Ten

Summary: In the Central London Hatchery and Conditioning Centre the Director tells Henry Foster that he is going to make a public example of Bernard in front of all the other colleagues. He accuses him of heretical views – this is in his opinion worse than murder, which kills only one person, whereas unorthodoxy undermines the very pillars of society. When Bernard nervously enters, the D.H.C. gives a speech attacking Bernard's abnormal behaviour in the fields of sports, sex, and *soma*. The D.H.C. declares his banishment to Iceland. Asked if he has anything to say in his defence, Bernard ushers Linda into the lab, evoking astonishment and horror. Linda

The D.H.C. tries to have Bernard exiled but instead is publicly humiliated by the arrival of his 'son', John.

immediately recognises the D.H.C., her former lover, whereas he does not, due to her sagging body and aged skin. When she hugs him and says that he made her the mother of a boy, he is horrified and turns pale. Then John comes in, kneels before him, and calls him 'my father'. This term of address, considered to be obscene, triggers roars of laughter at the Director's expense. Utterly humiliated, he rushes from the room.

Commentary: Chapter Ten begins with a description of the procedures in the Hatchery, which serves to remind the reader of what has been described in some detail at the beginning of the novel. At the same time it contrasts the Reservation with the civilized world in preparation for the clash of their cultures that is about to follow.

The D.H.C. plans to banish Bernard to Iceland for his 'unorthodoxy of behaviour'. Since individual opinions threaten the stability of society, he wants Bernard's punishment to serve as a deterrent to the upper-caste workers of the hatchery. He repeats in his speech the central values of society.

However, Bernard turns the tables by bringing in the D.H.C.'s hideously aged lover and natural son, both of whom cast an indecent and ridiculous light on the D.H.C. It is interesting to note that the D.H.C. has not broken any rules – it is simply that his reputation has been destroyed by the unexpected consequences of his behaviour, which have placed him outside the conformist norms of society. This is particularly remarkable as at the beginning of the chapter he was a powerful representative of the system.

Chapter Eleven

Summary: The scene in the Central London Hatchery and Conditioning Centre completely changes the lives of the characters. Upper-caste London longs to see the man who called the Director his 'father'. The D.H.C. himself immediately resigned from his post in shame. Linda on the other hand does not arouse any interest – people are appalled and revolted by her appearance and by the fact that she is a mother. She withdraws to Bernard's flat, where she indulges in a permanent *soma* holiday. Although a doctor warns John about the dangers of taking *soma* in high doses over a long period, John finally has to accept Linda's drug consumption. The alternative would be having to put up with Linda screaming for *soma* all the time due to her inability to face reality.

John becomes a famous person who everyone wants to meet.

Linda takes soma on a permanent basis.

As Bernard controls access to John, he suddenly finds himself, for the first time in his life, being treated as a person of '*outstanding importance*' (p. 134, l. 15). Comments about his abnormal appearance cease, people who used to deride him now treat him in a friendly way, and he can have any woman he likes. He feels '*lighter than air*' and '*gigantic*' (p. 135, ll. 31, 30). His success reconciles him with many aspects of the World State of which he had previously been critical. However, he now believes he has the right to criticize the system in order to reinforce his individuality and importance. Behind his back people predict his eventual downfall due to his self-important attitude. Even Helmholtz Watson is distressed by Bernard's development, which Bernard misinterprets as envy. He decides to end his friendship with Helmholtz.

Bernard becomes popular, as people can only gain access to John through him.

The World Controller's letter of recommendation enables Bernard to show John many aspects of the World State. John's reactions, though, are not what Bernard had hoped for and expected. While visiting a factory, John is disgusted by an 83-member Bokanovsky Group. At the upper-caste school Eton, John sits in on a geography lesson about the Reservation, whose customs and traditions make the pupils laugh. When John asks the Head Mistress about the teaching of Shakespeare, she tells him that modern education does not encourage students to seek solitary amusements.

John is not impressed by civilization.

In intermittent reports to Mustapha Mond, Bernard informs the World Controller about John's progress. He writes that, contrary to expectations, John does not respond to civilization with astonishment or awe. John's refusal to take *soma* puzzles Bernard, as does his close relationship to Linda. Mond is offended by Bernard's lecturing tone and his criticism of the system: the World Controller plans to teach Bernard a lesson in due time.

John has changed Lenina's life as well. She is now courted by many people. She confides to her friend Fanny that she finds John very attractive, but she has to admit that she has not yet had sex with him because he avoids her. In an elated mood Lenina looks forward to going to the feelies with John in the evening. The erotic feely, accompanied by a scent organ and a synthetic music machine, is about a black man who loses his conditioning in a helicopter accident and develops a passion for one woman only, but in the end is re-programmed to have polygamous relationships. Whereas Lenina enjoys herself and sees the film as the overture to a night with John, he is horrified by the shallow and pornographic plot, and leaves her weeping in front of her apartment. John returns to Bernard's flat and reads Shakespeare's *Othello*, which was brought to mind by the black protagonist of the feely.

Lenina starts to have strong feelings for John, who refuses – to her dismay – to have sex with her.

Commentary: John's appearance in the civilized world has an enormous effect on the lives of all the main characters. Bernard seems to be the winner in the new situation. His personal enemy, the D.H.C., has been destroyed. Bernard's popularity as John's guardian has increased enormously, particularly with women. The promiscuity he indulges in highlights the hypocrisy of his former criticism of the society's sexual norms, as his criticism was due to the lack of opportunities to enjoy promiscuity himself. To keep his self-respect and self-image as a sort of rebel, he continues criticizing the system, e.g. in his reports to the World Controller Mond. But the reader knows from Helmholtz's reaction, and from Mond's comments, that Bernard's present situation will not last, based as it is not on character but on luck. Ironically, in his reports Bernard accuses John of abnormal social behaviour (his refusal to take *soma* and his deep relationship with his mother), which recalls the criticism to which he himself had been subject.

Bernard comes across as hypocritical.

The reader learns that Bernard's popularity is superficial through the change in narrative perspective, as we get to see the thoughts and words of other people in society.

Lenina's popularity has also grown, as people are curious to know what the Savage is like – and especially what sex with the Savage is like. However, she is confused by John's treatment of her. She feels that there is a mutual attraction, but his reserve is incomprehensible to someone who has been conditioned to gratify their desires at once. Their visit to the feely ends in a deep disappointment for her when John leaves her alone instead of having intercourse with her. Her only way to deal with this rejection is by taking *soma*.

John is the new star of society, as everyone wants to meet him. Yet his popularity is due to his freak value. His values and ideas may be interesting for a short time, but they will inevitably lead him into conflict with the World State. Huxley uses John as an instrument for the reader to view developments in society from the point of view of the naïve outsider, which is a popular device in utopian literature. For that reason Huxley shows John's reaction to the factory, where the similarity of the Bokanovsky Group makes him vomit; to Eton (the school Huxley attended), where he finds the shallowness of the education offensive; and to the feely, which he finds horrible because of its pornographic, primitive plot. The fact that Lenina loves this kind of entertainment and wants to have sex with him immediately afterwards makes him shrink back from her: he wants her to be something special for him, and wants to prove himself worthy of her. The conflict between their value systems prevents them from coming together, despite this being what both wish for. While Lenina takes refuge in *soma*, John finds comfort in Shakespeare. It is difficult to imagine how the relationship will develop.

Linda is unable to cope with her role as a despised outcast in the World State. The only solution for her is long-term, life-threatening *soma* use. But even John has to accept grudgingly that her life would be even worse without it; her conditioning denies her the personal resources needed to deal with her problems. Only John still cares for her in a world where old age has no place.

Chapter Twelve

Summary: After being treated too long like a circus freak, John refuses to appear at a party Bernard has organized for a very distinguished crowd. The party is therefore a total failure, as everyone was there just to meet John. Bernard is talked about in very negative terms, especially by the Arch-Community-Songster, the leading religious representative, who indignantly leaves the event to spend the night with Lenina. Lenina has unusually strong feelings about John, who is shut up in his room, reading *Romeo and Juliet*. When she is together with the Arch-Community-Songster, she still thinks of John and takes *soma* to ease her mind.

John's refusal to attend a party with dignitaries leads to Bernard's social downfall.

The World Controller censors a paper dealing with the purpose of human life. Despite acknowledging the author's ingenuity and the potential importance of the paper, for the sake of social stability he cannot accept any search for a meaning of life beyond instant happiness. In fact, Mustapha Mond personally regards a deeper meaning of life as possible, but cannot allow a public discussion of this topic.

After the disastrous party, Bernard's buoyant self-confidence vanishes and gives way to his old self-pity. In this situation John and Helmholtz prove to be his true friends. Nevertheless, Bernard is angry with and resentful of them both – John because of his refusal to join the party, which has led to Bernard's fall from favour, Helmholtz because of his generosity and lack of reproaches, which makes Bernard feel even more ashamed of himself.

In the meantime Helmholtz has written a poem on the positive aspect of solitude which brings him into conflict with his superior, as this attitude contradicts the fundamental belief that solitude should be avoided. Helmholtz feels a power inside him that is about to erupt. He and John take to one another at once, which makes Bernard jealous. When they recite poetry to each other, Bernard destroys the solemn atmosphere by making derisive remarks. But even Helmholtz bursts out laughing as John reads out a passage from *Romeo and Juliet* in which Juliet begs her mother not to make her marry a man she does not love. Helmholtz's conditioning does not allow him to understand Juliet's desperate situation, although he realizes that a person has to encounter extreme distress in order to produce great poetry. John is disappointed by Helmholtz's reaction, even more so since he identifies himself and Lenina with the protagonists of the tragedy.

Helmholtz gets into trouble with the authorities.

Helmholtz and John become good friends.

Commentary: The disaster at the party reveals how hollow Bernard's new self-assurance is. His old inferiority complex returns. He is too shallow to understand his role in the new situation. It is interesting to note that the kind of behaviour shown by Bernard and his guests is not so very different from social behaviour in our own society. Bernard discovers that he does have two sincere friends, John and Helmholtz, who prefer the real Bernard, insecure as he may be, to the boasting braggart. Bernard, however, reveals his pettiness in wanting to take revenge on these two friends who treat him so generously.

John and Helmholtz like each other and share an appreciation of poetical language. Helmholtz is no longer satisfied with the shallow texts he has to produce for his job and longs for more substantial matter. Writing a poem celebrating solitude provokes a warning from his boss to

In the novel one can only understand life through solitude.

refrain from such subversive topics that contradict the state's official ideals. His efforts to express individual experience and emotions make him more and more of an outsider, who, like John and Bernard before him, longs for a challenge to fully explore his potential. It is worth noting that, even in a society as controlled and conditioned as the World State, it is still possible for people (although probably only Alphas) to develop their own consciousness and individuality.

John, untouched by the social conditioning of the World State, has feelings towards Lenina which in their depth resemble the feelings that Helmholtz is searching for. In Shakespeare's *Romeo and Juliet* he finds adequate expression for his own situation, while the end of the drama foreshadows the tragic ending of the novel. Lenina attempts to transcend her conditioning and environment, driven by her genuine feeling for John, but her education makes her incapable of either expressing her feelings or consciously wishing for anything but immediate gratification.

Mustapha Mond, the World Controller, stands above all that. With interest and understanding he reads a paper on the purpose of life. For him it does indeed seem possible that there could be a meaning to life beyond permanent and immediate happiness and physical well-being, for instance *'some intensification and refining of consciousness, some enlargement of knowledge'* (p. 152, ll. 17–18). Yet no matter what his personal convictions may be, he will always act in the best interests of the state. Chapters 16 and 17 offer philosophical discussions between Mond and John, the only characters in the novel who are capable of truly independent thought because they possess knowledge.

Chapter Thirteen

Summary: Lenina has fallen in love with John, leading her to reject Henry Foster's invitation to the feelies. She discusses her situation with Fanny; her friend, however, is unable to understand why Lenina does not just follow her desire like everybody else. In the end, Fanny persuades Lenina to take some *soma* to give her the courage to go to John and 'take' him.

When Lenina arrives at Bernard's apartment, John is thinking about his feelings for Lenina, too. They come closer to each other, John quoting lines from Shakespeare about the perfection of the beloved woman. But just before they kiss, John recoils, telling Lenina that he wants to prove himself worthy of her, which she cannot understand. He confesses his love, and talks about marriage – a ghastly prospect for Lenina, meaning she would have to stay with one man for the rest of her life. Finally, she takes the initiative, begins to caress him tenderly, and starts to undress. John is reminded of the pornographic feely they watched together and violently rejects her, calling her a whore and threatening to kill her. Lenina flees in panic to the bathroom and locks herself in. Then the telephone rings, and she overhears one side of a conversation that makes John leave the flat at once. Still afraid, Lenina runs away.

Lenina tries to have sex with John, who reacts violently.

Commentary: This chapter is about love, and the various attitudes to love experienced and felt by the characters. John and Lenina are attracted to each other, but the fundamental differences in their conditioning and attitudes means their love is doomed to failure. Having grown up in a traditional social environment and having been inspired by Shakespeare, John holds on to the ideals of romantic love, whereas Lenina simply yearns for the fulfilment of her sexual desires. Lenina does in fact develop feelings for John that far exceed the normal promiscuous and carefree attitude of society. Considered unusual for her attachments by her friends, she is considered too promiscuous by John.

From a modern point of view John's attitude towards sex seems quite radical, but for Huxley and his contemporaries John behaves more or less according to prevailing contemporary moral standards, which in a time before the contraceptive pill was invented condemned extramarital sex. Yet it was also a time in which moral norms were being challenged, and sexual relations, especially among the liberal upper classes to which Huxley belonged, were becoming more permissive and less bound to traditional ideas of monogamy and love (i.e. marriage).

In this violent scene, the author shows that neither Lenina's nor John's approach to sex is good.

There is also a good deal of humour in this chapter. John wants to prove his worthiness through noble actions. First, he wants to kill a lion for Lenina, but unfortunately there are no lions in England. Then he is prepared to humiliate himself by sweeping the floor, yet Lenina can't understand why he would want to, as there are vacuum cleaners and Epsilons to operate them. Another instance of humour is the contrast between Shakespeare's love lyrics and the blunt exhortations and titillations of the World State's poetry.

Chapter Fourteen

Summary: In Park Lane Hospital for the Dying people who are about to die spend their final hours under the influence of incessant joyful

John visits his dying mother.

music, television sets which are never turned off, and a constantly shifting programme of perfumes, all of which are intended to create a pleasant atmosphere. This is where Linda is dying. John's emotional state puzzles the nurses, for whom death is nothing terrible – the dying individuals and their loss do not really matter to anyone.

John finds his mother dozing and barely conscious. Watching Linda die makes him remember beautiful moments of his youth. Suddenly a shrill noise tears him from his memories. A Bokanovsky group of eight-year-olds happily enters the room for a lesson in death-conditioning. Accustomed as they are to never-aging faces, they are appalled and disgusted by Linda. When John indignantly reacts to their disgusted shock, he is warned by the nurse not to interfere with death-conditioning or he will be removed from the room.

John tries to recall pleasant memories from his childhood, but can now only recall hateful memories connected with Popé's intrusion into his life. When Linda mistakes him for Popé, John becomes furious and shakes Linda; she stops breathing and dies. Reproaching himself for having killed her, he falls on his knees and weeps. The nurse fears the effect this may have on the children's death-conditioning and immediately offers them chocolate éclairs, which distracts them from John's unusual behaviour. In his grief John appeals to God, and then leaves.

John is upset that his mother dies without acknowledging him. He is equally upset that death is treated as though it were nothing special.

Commentary: Whereas the previous chapter deals with love, this one examines death. As before, such a fundamental issue brings about a further violent clash between John and the World State.

Love and grief are two strong emotions that are prohibited in the World State.

As the World State does not accept individuality, the death of a single person is of little importance. People in the World State die as they live, '*in company and with all the modern conveniences*' (p. 171, l. 10) such as happy synthetic melodies, a TV to distract them from deeper thoughts, and constant stimulation from perfumes. Death-conditioning teaches children not to view the end of life as something sad. They are shown that even the dying display no traces of physical ageing or suffering. Games and chocolate make death just another enjoyable experience for the children. As described in Chapter Five, the bodies of the deceased are recycled as a final service for society.

For John, the death of his mother is one of the most moving moments of his life. He is overwhelmed by emotion and recalls conflicting memories from the past. Of course, he is deeply disappointed when his mother mistakes him for Popé, the person he hated most as a boy. But he is even more shocked at the indifference of the nurses and the lack of respect of the children. In that moment of grief and helplessness in the face of death, John takes refuge in religion and calls for God.

John's mother's sexual partner is more important to her than her own son.

For Huxley, the individuality of life is inextricably bound to the individuality of death. His description of an impersonal death therefore completes his criticism of a life spent in shallow amusements and infantile gratifications. Huxley points here to a trend towards excluding the unpleasant reality of death from everyday life, a tendency that has become even stronger since *Brave New World* was written. Huxley saw his own mother die from cancer when he was 14, which strongly influenced his attitude towards death.

Chapter Fifteen

Summary: On leaving the hospital, John has to pass through a crowd of Deltas who are waiting for their daily *soma* ration. Their sameness appals him – they remind him of maggots. Miranda's words from Shakespeare's *The Tempest* – 'How beauteous mankind is! O brave new world!' – have a mocking and cynical ring for John in the face of those repulsively identical Deltas. But then Miranda's words change their meaning for John; he hears in them instead a call for action to transform this society into a genuinely beautiful world. John feels the urge to bring freedom to the creatures of the World State.

John tries to prevent a crowd of Deltas from having their soma rations, thereby almost creating a riot.

John interrupts the *soma* distribution and delivers a speech to the Deltas in which he warns them that *soma* is poison, and promises them freedom and the end of slavery. The *soma* distributor phones Bernard and Helmholtz, who immediately hurry to the hospital. When they arrive, they watch John throwing the *soma* pills out of the window. At first the Deltas are shocked into immobility, but then they start moving towards John menacingly. Helmholtz helps John fight them off while Bernard does nothing and wrings his hands at the edge of the fight, wanting to help his friends but scared of joining in. Before he comes to a decision, the police rush in and end the turmoil with the help of *soma* vapour, a powerful anaesthetic, and a recorded appeal to be '*happy and good together*' (p.185, ll.28–29) again. John and Helmholtz are arrested, as is Bernard, despite his cowardly inactivity and attempt to escape.

Helmholtz and Bernard arrive; Helmholtz tries to support John, while Bernard does not get involved.

Commentary: The stark contrast between his feelings after Linda's death and the superficial world in which he finds himself drives John to take action. The Shakespeare quotation 'brave new world' has acquired a new meaning for John. Having initially been a kind of promise, when John was about to leave the Reservation for the beautiful world which his mother had told him stories about, the words have become in the face of the reality of the World State a cynical comment on a world that has replaced real beauty and experience with superficiality. In the final step, John interprets Miranda's words as his mission in this world: to make something beautiful and transform *'the nightmare into something fine and noble'* (p. 181, ll. 29–30).

John realizes that *soma* is the basis of the mental slavery he despises, which is why he seizes the opportunity to disrupt *soma* distribution to the Delta workers. Of course, his efforts to liberate the masses are doomed to failure – the masses are conditioned both to be dependent and to love that very dependence, while their critical faculties are too underdeveloped to understand what John is offering them. John's speech culminates in the exclamation *'I'll* make *you be free whether you want to or not'* (p. 184, ll. 6–7), a indication that freedom is not always what the oppressed seek; they may indeed prefer the comfort and security of slavery. Helmholtz joins John in his attempt to free the people, maybe because he recognizes that this could be the challenge he has been longing for. In a scene that recalls Peter's denial of Jesus in the New Testament, Bernard tries to escape, but finally stands by his friends and is also arrested.

At the close of the chapter the reader is in suspense, wondering how the World State is going to deal with its opponents – the protagonists.

Chapter Sixteen

Summary: The three men are brought to Mustapha Mond's study. When the Controller asks John if he likes civilization, the savage bluntly answers that he does not, despite its seemingly pleasant aspects.

Mond replies with a quotation from Shakespeare, which is the starting point of a discussion about the role of the poet in the World State. He explains that Shakespeare is forbidden (except to people like himself, who make the laws) because his works are old and beautiful and the World State's controllers *'don't want people to be attracted by old things. We want them to like the new ones'* (p. 188, ll. 32–33). Moreover, Mond points out that people would not understand a drama like *Othello*, because an appreciation of tragedy requires a different, unstable world, of the kind which has been long since abolished. The sacrifice of beauty and high art was the price that had to be paid for stability and happiness. Mond concedes that the shallow entertainment they offer is not as spectacular as the conflicts with misfortune, temptation and emotions: *'Happiness is never grand'* (p. 190, l. 29).

Mond discusses the reasons why the World State was set up.

Art has been sacrificed for stability and happiness.

When John remarks how repulsive he finds the identical twins of Bokanovsky Groups, the conversation shifts to aspects of the social order. John asks why they do not engineer everybody to become an Alpha Plus. The Controller explains that an Alpha would go mad if he had to do lower caste work, whereas lower castes are conditioned to love their menial labour. Mond tells John of an experiment conducted in A.F. 473: the island of Cyprus was colonized with 22,000 Alphas, who were left to themselves. Since nobody wanted to

The caste system ensures that everyone is happy with their work.

do menial labour, strikes, disobedience and intrigues soon led to a bloody civil war. The survivors asked the World Controllers to resume the government of the island, which promptly ended the experiment.

Mond claims that '*the optimum population is modelled on the iceberg – eight-ninths below the water line, one-ninth above*' (p. 192, ll. 26–27). To his mind, the people below are happier than those above because work, entertainment and *soma* provide them with all they need. Another test in Ireland showed that a reduction of working hours, which would be technically feasible, would lead to unrest and an increased consumption of *soma* because the workers were incapable of actually enjoying more free time. Therefore longer working hours contribute to people's happiness, and simultaneously to the stability of the state.

Science serves only to ensure the stability of the state.

Another achievement that had to be sacrificed was the unlimited pursuit of science. While people are taught through hypnopaedia that '*science is everything*' (p. 194, l. 4), Mond explains that it has been given narrow scope for development – unrestricted science is a potential danger to stability. He himself was a good physicist in his youth, but his unorthodox studies brought him close to being sent to an island.

As soon as the subject of banishment to an island is brought up, Bernard tries to exculpate himself by blaming John and Helmholtz for what happened in the hospital. He begins to weep, falls on his knees before the Controller, and begs not to be banished to Iceland. Mond finally has him carried out and treated with *soma*. He then makes it clear to Helmholtz why being exiled is more of a reward than a punishment: the interesting people – individuals with thought-provoking ideas – live together on the islands, free from the conformist constrictions of the World State. However, as a young man Mond sacrificed his interest in pure science and preferred to stay in civilization, exchanging personal fulfilment for the chance to exercise power.

Mond then looks back to the beginning of the 20th century, when people expected science to expand indefinitely, when knowledge and truth were the supreme values. However, Ford himself helped to precipitate the change towards comfort and happiness through the mass production he helped introduce. The Nine Years' War made it clear that unlimited scientific progress leads to destabilization and destruction. In the aftermath of the War, the use and study of science became restricted to creating a state of happiness.

Helmholtz and Bernard are exiled.

When the Controller asks Helmholtz which island he would like to be exiled to, he asks for one with an unpleasant climate, which he believes will inspire him to create better literature. Then he goes to look after Bernard, leaving Mustapha Mond and John alone.

Commentary: This and the following chapter are the philosophical climax of the novel, and involve discussions of essential values like beauty, as embodied by Shakespeare, truth, in the form of science, and happiness. Mustapha Mond is the mouthpiece of the system who believes that that the emphasis has shifted '*from truth and beauty to comfort and happiness*' (p. 196, ll. 9–10), but it is clear that his private opinions clash with his responsibilities as a leader of the state, which makes him sound somewhat cynical. Many of the developments discussed here are reflections of changes that were taking place during Huxley's lifetime (cf. pp. 87ff. and 97ff. of this book).

In this chapter, the characters are not the main focus. Mustapha Mond is hardly characterized at all – what he has to say is more important than his actual character.

Helmholtz sees banishment as an opportunity to discover more about himself. Bernard by contrast is devastated. He used to flatter his self-image by imagining himself in the role of a rebel, but his actions repeatedly reveal that his '*theoretical courage*' (p.89, l.26) was based on his inability to enjoy the pleasures of society without scruples. When exile on a distant island threatens his comfort, he cowardly betrays his friends and begs for mercy in a most abject manner. Both Helmholtz and Bernard stay true to their characters as the reader met them at the beginning of the novel: Helmholtz is strong-willed and worthy of the admiration that he has received from others, while Bernard is a snivelling, spineless manipulator, unworthy of respect.

It may be considered a weakness in the novel that Huxley seems more interested in philosophical discussion than in plot, but in every utopian novel there must be some discussion about the rationale behind and the history of the utopian society.

Chapter Seventeen

Mond explains why religion plays no real role in society.

Summary: Mustapha Mond and John continue their debate about values. Mond says that in addition to art and science, religion was also abolished after the Nine Years' War. From a safe in his office he takes out forbidden books on religion and philosophy, including the Bible. The World Controller argues that religion is a compensation for hardships and miseries, especially those of old age. There is consequently no place for God in a world in which everybody is young and all desires can be immediately gratified. When John objects that God's existence is independent of human beings, Mond claims that there might be a God who *'manifests himself as an absence; as though he weren't there at all'* (p.201, ll.21–22). John contends that it is natural to believe in God, particularly when one is alone. Mond replies that people only believe in things they have been conditioned to believe, and that nobody is ever alone in the new World State. John argues that there has to be a God to punish and reward human behaviour, that God is the reason for all things noble and heroic, including patience, courage, self-denial and chastity. The Controller responds that everybody is perfect and that there is no need or place for heroism in a world with neither hardship nor deferment of gratification.

The Savage accuses the World State of *'getting rid of everything unpleasant instead of learning to put up with it'* (p.205, ll.11–12). People must pay a price in order to be able to value things, and sometimes they need the risk and the adrenaline rush of living dangerously; but the World State regularly satisfies this human need with the Violent Passion Surrogate.

The discussion culminates in John's exclamation that he does not want comfort, *'I want God, I want poetry, I want real danger, I want freedom, I want goodness. I want sin.'* (p.206, ll.16–17). For the World Controller this means *'claiming the right to be unhappy'* (p.206, ll.18–19). John is prepared to accept that price.

Commentary: This chapter deals with the topic of religion, which like art and science has been rendered obsolete in a world in which people experience no hardship. It is interesting to note that it is common in utopian literature for an intelligent leader to have knowledge of the past. This knowledge facilitates powerful arguments against the old order. Although Mond's personal convictions remain in the background, he shows some sympathy for John's arguments, which again makes his own argumentation often seem cynical.

The discussions of values in Chapters Sixteen and Seventeen make it clear that Huxley's utopia is meant to be understood as a dystopia. While John struggles to argue using clichés and sentimental concepts from the old world, Mond succinctly shows how fitting, functional and even necessary the World State's methodology and approach is in this new world. Yet the simplistic clarity of Mond's arguments cannot help but raise doubts in the reader's mind.

It is interesting to note that the discussion ends with a shrug of the shoulders, which indicates indifference – an unusual reaction for a World Controller.

The end of the debate leaves an unbridgeable gap between the World Controller, who defends the order of his state, and John, who prefers to live life to the full, even if this involves embracing pain, difficulties and disadvantages.

Chapter Eighteen

Summary: When Helmholtz and Bernard come to John's apartment to say good-bye, they find him vomiting after drinking mustard and warm water in order to purify himself, like the Indians do. Bernard apologizes for his behaviour the day before. John informs them that he asked the Controller if he could join his friends on the islands, but Mond refused, saying that he wants '*to go on with the experiment*' (p.208, l.19). John, however, is resolved to leave civilization and seek solitude.

John's behaviour reverts to that he learned in the Reservation.

John decides to seek out solitude.

The next day he finds an abandoned air-lighthouse some kilometres away from London. After a sleepless night spent in prayer and flagellation, including once again his endurance test in imitation of the crucifixion, he feels he has earned the right to inhabit the lighthouse. As a hermit he enjoys the solitude, he makes a bow and arrows and is delighted *'to be doing something that demanded skill and patience'* (p.212, ll.4–5). When he becomes aware that he is singing at work, he feels guilty for being happy and carefree; he savagely whips himself to punish himself for this weakness. While doing this he is observed by some Deltas, who alert others to John's strange (and, for them, exciting) behaviour.

Crowds of pleasure seekers visit John due to his habit of whipping himself.

Three days later swarms of reporters arrive at the lighthouse and try to interview him. John reacts with increasing violence. Left in peace for some days, John recalls Lenina, a seductive memory for which he wants to punish himself. While whipping himself, he is filmed secretly by a wildlife photographer. When the film is broadcast as *The Savage of Surrey*, new interest is aroused, and masses swarm to the lighthouse. Fascinated by the vicarious thrill and horror of pain, the spectators demand the *'whipping stunt'*. Lenina's arrival increases John's rage and he starts whipping her and himself, to the amusement of the masses. The spectacle ends in an orgy, in which John also takes part. When he awakens and remembers what he has done, John utters his final words *'Oh, my God, my God'* (p.222, l.11) in despair.

John's participation in the orgy makes him realize he will never find peace of mind in this society.

When the curious spectators return, they find John in the lighthouse, hanging from the ceiling.

Commentary: The final chapter shows how John consistently follows his path to the very end. He withdraws from society and punishes himself mercilessly to atone for the pleasures he enjoys. His imitation of Jesus's crucifixion and his final words allude to the New Testament, giving these scenes in particular, and his role in the novel in general, a strong religious undertone.

His extraordinary behaviour becomes an attraction for the masses, so that the only way for him to find peace is to kill himself. Of course, John's radicalism seems strange, but without it the fundamental contrast to the World State would have been incomplete. Confronted by the curiosity and lust for sensation of the masses, people who stick to the 'old' values of beauty, truth and religion stand no chance.

The Characters

Bernard Marx

Name	allusion to: • George **Bernard** Shaw (1856–1950), an influential Irish writer with strong socialist convictions. • Karl **Marx** (1818–1883), German political philosopher, whose ideas about the role of the working class became the theoretical basis of a worldwide workers' movement (called socialism, communism or Marxism), which finally led to the Russian Revolution in 1917. Marx demanded the abolition of private property and the economic and political equality of all citizens.
Job	psychologist (p. 75, l. 19), specialist on hypnopaedia in the Central London Hatchery and Conditioning Centre (p. 43, l. 5)
Caste	Alpha Plus
Description	small (normally a sign of being a member of a lower caste); thin body and melancholy face (p. 50, ll. 12–13); his physique is '*hardly better than that of the average Gamma*' (p. 56, ll. 11–12). There are rumours that somebody accidentally put '*alcohol into his blood-surrogate*' (p. 42, ll. 22–23).

There is no character in the novel whose role in the story and whose assessment by the reader change as much as that of Bernard Marx. In the first half of the novel Huxley builds him up as the protagonist.

The way Bernard is introduced in the novel provides an ironic comment on the perfect world order, occurring as it does just as the Controller is explaining how the state has eliminated unpleasant feelings like love, jealousy, etc. Bernard seems to have all these feelings within him. Indeed, Bernard seems to be the only imperfect person in a perfect world, as he physically resembles a Gamma while intellectually he is an Alpha-Plus. This discrepancy leads to rumours about him having been given too much alcohol in his blood surrogate during production. His physical imperfection leads to a lack of self-confidence, which is revealed in his contact with lower-caste people. Fearing that they might not respect him because of his physical inferiority, he treats them arrogantly as he *'does not feel himself too secure in his superiority'* (p. 56, ll. 6–7).

Bernard's physical peculiarity is matched by his unusual behaviour. He prefers to be alone, despises popular entertainments like the feelies, and is disgusted by the way other men talk about Lenina, *'as though she were a bit of meat'* (p. 42, l. 5). In a way, Bernard is trapped in a vicious circle: he feels like an outsider, and *'feeling an outsider he behaved like one'* (p. 56, ll. 24–25) – which, in turn, reinforces both other people's prejudices and his own feeling of loneliness. His role as an outcast makes him hate (and fear) self-confident men like Henry Foster, his rival for Lenina, and Benito Hoover – men who move *'through the caste system as a fish through water'* (p. 56, l. 33). Bernard also hates and resents society as a whole, which has put him in this unpleasant situation.

In Chapter Five, Part Two, a scene depicting the Solidarity Service (a caricature of Christian religious services) demonstrates clearly how Bernard is excluded from 'normal' social amusements. The rite culminates in a *soma*-and-sex orgy in which everybody attains union with 'the Greater Being' – except for Bernard, who just pretends to experience the same as the other participants. His self-consciousness prevents him from sharing the ecstasy, and reminds him painfully of his position as outsider.

Lenina finds him attractive precisely because of his smallness – she wants to stroke him *'like a cat'* (p. 42, l. 20). Nevertheless, their dates are always marked by a huge gap in their expectations. For the polygamous Lenina, Bernard is only one relationship among many. Although she does like him, she is merely looking for the same thing she seeks with other men: fun (anything else would deviate from her conditioning). Bernard also offers her the opportunity of travelling to the Reservation, which could be a new and exciting experience.

For Bernard their relationship is different; for his part, real feelings seem to be involved. When he meets her in the elevator, Bernard is shy and blushes. Contrary to a lifetime of hypnopaedic slogans, he wants to be alone with her *'for talking'* (p.76, l.27), something Lenina can't understand. Neither does she understand his refusal to take soma to cheer himself up: instead he insists *'I'd rather be myself. Myself and nasty. Not somebody else, however jolly.'* (p.77, ll.8–10). His desire not to be *'just a cell in the social body'* and not to be *'enslaved by my conditioning'* (p.78, ll.8, 21) is horrible and shocking, even a *'blasphemy'* (p.78, l.16) to her. Her inability to understand his thoughts and needs finally forces him to take *soma* and have sex with her, for fear of losing her for good. His attempts *'to try the effect of arresting my impulses, […] to know what passion is, […] to feel something strongly'* (p.80, ll.21–22, 28–29) fail because Lenina is not a partner with whom he can share his feelings.

On the trip to the Reservation with Lenina, Bernard is looking for life unspoiled by conditioning, progress and civilization. Bernard tries to understand the Indian way of life as an alternative to the civilized world in which he feels ill at ease. As Lenina has a violently negative reaction to the Reservation, ultimately their affair comes to an end.

The trip to the Reservation terminates not only Bernard's relationship with Lenina, but also with the Director of Hatcheries. The D.H.C. has observed Bernard's abnormal and unorthodox behaviour suspiciously for a long time. Bernard's competence at his job (p.76, ll.8–9) saves him from being fired, but the D.H.C. warns him that he will be sent to Iceland if there are any more complaints about him. This threat has an unexpected effect on Bernard. Instead of being intimidated, he feels heroic, fighting *'against the order of things; elated by the intoxicating consciousness of his individual significance and importance'* (p.84, ll.26–27). The Director's threat is the great trial he has been waiting for to prove his strength and his character (although he does not really take the threat seriously). But when it comes to the test, when he finds out in the Reservation that the D.H.C has decided to banish him to Iceland, *'of that imagined stoicism, that theoretical courage, not a trace was left'* (p.89, ll.25–26).

Bernard sees the D.H.C. as an unjust superior as well as a representative of the society in which he feels inferior. As soon as he realizes that John is the Director's son, Bernard develops a plan to take revenge on the D.H.C by taking John and Linda to London with the World Controller's permission. His strategy succeeds: just as the D.H.C. is accusing Bernard of unorthodox behaviour and proclaiming his banishment to Iceland in front of the whole staff, Bernard presents the D.H.C. with his son John and his former lover Linda, thereby humiliating the D.H.C., who resigns from his post. This victory is a turning point for Bernard within the story: John replaces him as the protagonist while the hollowness and superficiality of his heroism and behaviour are revealed.

John changes society's awareness of Bernard, and Bernard's own self-perception. As John's *'accredited guardian'* (p. 134, l. 13), Bernard is now treated as a *'person of outstanding importance'* (p. 134, l. 15) and becomes popular among people who ignored or despised him before. Most importantly for him, Bernard can have any woman he wants, and makes ample use of this opportunity. He boasts to Helmholtz about his sexual deeds. *'Success went fizzily to Bernard's head'* (p. 135, l. 13).

His behaviour proves that his former feelings about not treating women like meat was not due in any way to his moral convictions, but was merely due to lack of opportunity. Hence it is no surprise that Bernard becomes *'reconciled by his success'* and suddenly finds *'the order of things was good'* (p. 135, ll. 16–17). He continues to criticize the system, but now merely to support his belief in his own superiority and to parade his self-importance. He is however only tolerated by the higher members of society as long as he can offer the spectacle of the Savage. So, while Bernard is feeling *'gigantic'* and like *'a visiting World Controller'* for the first time in his life, his critics predict his impending downfall. Indeed, offended by Bernard's arrogant attitude, Mustapha Mond has earmarked him for a lesson to bring him down to earth again.

How hollow Bernard's success is becomes clear when John refuses to appear at a party to which Bernard has invited a lot of people to meet the Savage. As soon as he informs his guests of John's refusal to make an appearance, they are furious and resentful of Bernard having wasted their time – his *'happy self-confidence'* (p. 150, l. 9) dwindles and *'what should have been the crowning moment of Bernard's whole career had turned out to be the moment of his greatest humiliation'* (p. 151, ll. 5–6).

This failure exposes again 'his old self', unhappy and lacking self-confidence.

Bernard's downward spiral continues with his involvement in the uproar at Park Lane Hospital. Whereas John and Helmholtz try to liberate the Deltas from *soma* (in vain, of course), Bernard hesitates about whether to help his friends or not. When the police eventually arrive, he cowardly seeks to save himself from being arrested – to no avail.

Taken to the World Controller's office, Bernard is completely crushed. Shocked by John's and Helmholtz's openness, he betrays his friends in order to exculpate himself. He starts crying and falls on his knees before the Controller, again revealing his cowardly character. His miserable behaviour obviously cannot prevent his exile. Bernard's desperation finally and completely reveals his hypocrisy – despite his criticism and resentment, he values the pleasures and comforts of civilization.

Bernard's friends John and Helmholtz forgive him his embarrassing behaviour when he apologizes to them, although Bernard has never been easy as a friend. What connects the three of them is their feeling of being individuals, which also makes them outsiders in society. With Helmholtz – although he is different in many respects – Bernard shares '*the knowledge that they were individuals*' (p. 58, ll. 24–25) and a certain dissatisfaction with their present situation. Helmholtz tolerates his friend's occasional fits of jealousy, self-pity, boasting, and his lack of pride, as he himself needs someone to listen to his problems.

Bernard's relationship with John is based on their feelings of loneliness and isolation from the people around them. When Bernard takes the Savage to London, it is not so much because of friendship and affection; Bernard plans to use the young man as an instrument of revenge against the D.H.C. And when John turns out to be a huge success in the civilized world, Bernard again employs John as a tool to improve his social acceptance.

When John refuses to serve Bernard's purposes, the relationship immediately changes. Bernard is angry at John and plans '*small revenges*' (p. 153, ll. 33f.) on him. Likewise, he sees Helmholtz as his '*victim-friend*' (p. 154, l. 8) who has to suffer the punishments which Bernard is unable to inflict on others. Ashamed of his own jealousy, he wants to *'take some revenge on Helmholtz for his generosity'* (p. 154, ll. 19–20). Bernard's envy grows when he notices that John and Helmholtz like each other more than they like him. He maliciously disturbs the harmonious atmosphere when his friends read poetry to one another. Ultimately, Bernard is a selfish, small-minded and hypocritical person, who fails to support his friends at the hospital and at the meeting with the World Controller.

Bernard Marx is a disappointing character: his moral standards turn out to have been formed by his feelings of resentment and frustration at having been rejected by society, and by his lack of opportunities to participate in "normal" social behaviour.

Revision
(what you learn about Bernard)

- Bernard is one of the main characters. At first he appears to be the protagonist, but as John becomes more important for the novel, Bernard's importance diminishes.
- Unlike the other characters, Bernard is a round character.
- Bernard moves the action forward by going to the Reservation, by finding John and bringing him back to London.
- He acts like a rebel who dislikes everything about his surroundings, but it becomes clear that he is merely reacting to his feelings of rejection by society.
- When he gains popularity, he feels more at home within the system.
- He lacks strength of character (for example, he needs to take *soma* when confronted with the possibility that he may be exiled to Iceland). When he is banished at the end he begs for mercy and blames the others.
- Although he wins the sympathy of the reader at first because he is an outsider fighting against the system, he slowly loses the respect of the reader as his true character become visible (especially when he returns to London after the Reservation).

Key passages	Analysis
p. 55, l. 10 – p. 57, l. 8 p. 118, ll. 1–3	Bernard's sense of inferiority is described here. He is an indecisive, small and ugly man who does not know how to talk to Lenina. Due to his lack of self-esteem he is arrogant and rude. He feels isolated from others.
p. 76, l. 11 – p. 79, l. 4 p. 80, l. 19 – p. 81, l. 10	Here we see Bernard trying to spend time alone with Lenina. He seems to rebel against the system by refusing to conform to social pressures, and questions the need for conditioning. He wants to feel things more intensely.
p. 84, l. 23 – p. 85, l. 19 p. 89, ll. 7–30	Bernard imagines that he has a strong rebellious nature, but we see that he is weak and insecure, incapable of dealing with adversity.
p. 128, ll. 13–24	The Director describes Bernard as a menace to society for refusing to conform to society's norms. The description is ironic, as Bernard is really rather cowardly.
p. 134, ll. 12–22 p. 135, ll. 3–31	Success goes to Bernard's head when he suddenly becomes someone of importance in society. We see that much of his rebelliousness was due to lack of opportunity rather than genuine unhappiness with the system.

Vocabulary: talking about Bernard Marx

enjoys being alone • lonely, insecure, self-pitying • low self-esteem • cowardly • lacking in pride • whinges/whines a lot • resentful of others non-conformist • feels alienated/excluded from society • takes pleasure in being different • enjoys playing the role of the rebel hypocritical • brags • boasts about himself • enjoys the feeling of being popular and successful • new-found popularity

John

Name	Most common name in the English language, therefore he functions as an Everyman. Also called 'the Savage' because he comes from the uncivilized Reservation.
Job	none
Caste	none (born naturally in the Reservation)
Description	*'his plaited hair was straw-coloured, his eyes a pale blue eyes, and his skin a white skin, bronzed'* (p. 99, ll. 29–30); *'such a nice-looking boy, and a really beautiful body'* (p. 100, ll. 28–29)

In his birth, upbringing, values and behaviour John is the opposite of everything that the World State stands for, to such an extent that his arrival in the civilized world is bound to lead to a catastrophe. John is modelled on the 'noble savage', a well-known figure in literature since the 18th century (cf. Jean Jacques Rousseau's *Émile*, Rudyard Kipling's Mowgli from *The Jungle Book*). The idea of the 'noble savage' is based on the concept that man has a natural goodness which is corrupted by civilization. He is often employed to view a society with the naïve or/and critical eyes of somebody who comes from outside.
John has been an outsider since his birth. His conception and birth are considered terrible accidents by his mother Linda. John's European complexion, his lack of a father, and his mother's reputation as an

alcoholic whore make him an outcast in Indian society. At times, John seems to share an equal status with the other Indian youths, for instance when he learns to work clay with the others at the age of 15. However, when the other adolescents undergo an initiation rite to become men, he is excluded because of his white parents and the reputation of his mother. Fleeing into the solitude of the desert and considering suicide, he *'discovered Time and Death and God'* (p. 117, l. 24), thereby becoming an adult in his own way. Likewise, his exclusion from other rites forces him to search for his own experiences, e.g. his imitation of Jesus on the cross (p. 118, ll. 16–17).

John's feelings of isolation are deep, and he introduces himself to Bernard and Lenina as *'a most unhappy gentleman'* (p. 100, ll. 1–2) and is overjoyed to have the chance to leave the Reservation with them. Influenced by Linda's stories about 'the Other Place' as a *'paradise of goodness and loveliness'* (p. 173, l. 27), John enters the civilized world with great expectations.

Civilization, however, turns out to be quite different from how he imagined it. Bernard is instructed to show John *'civilized life in all its aspects'* (p. 136, l. 5). John *'shows surprisingly little astonishment at, or awe of, civilized inventions'* (p. 136, ll. 19–20), as Bernard reports to the World Controller. Visiting an electrical equipment factory, for instance, John vomits at the sight of identical Bokanovsky twins. He is singularly unimpressed by the technology of the feelies. Moreover, he refuses to take *soma* because he would *'rather be unhappy than have the sort of false, lying happiness'* (p. 153, ll. 22–23) of the World State.

In his reports, Bernard explains John's behaviour with his *'being focussed on what he calls "the soul"'* (p. 136, l. 25). This is why the Savage is disappointed by his visit to Eton, where the pupils are taught the slogans of the World State instead of Shakespeare, and is horrified by the feely, as he misses depth and real emotions in the story. At home, he takes refuge in the violent passions of *Othello*.

John's relationship with his mother Linda is a troubled one. Her conditioning prevented her from being a good mother, as she has no notion of motherhood. Yet John feels love and respect for her, even though she withdraws from him as soon as she is in London and retreats into soma. John's love for her and his frequent visits astonish Bernard, who believes that the natural impulse is *'to recoil from an unpleasant object*' (p. 138, l. 23). John's deeply-felt grief at his mother's deteriorating condition and her subsequent death contrasts strongly with the aseptic atmosphere of the hospital, the indifference of the nurses, and the uniform joyfulness of the children who are being death-conditioned. This contrast triggers John's violent revolt against the system.

John's relationship with Lenina is rather complicated. For John it is love at first sight. He is fi lled with rapture when he sees Lenina sleeping; he uses Shakespeare's words to express the passionate feelings which he is experiencing for the fi rst time. Their love, however, is doomed to fail since their concepts of love are so different. Whereas Lenina does feel affection, she, like everybody else in the World State, sees relationships as temporary affairs based solely on sex. John, on the other hand, believes in eternal love and monogamy. Because Lenina does not understand this idea of love, John becomes aggressive and threatening when she tries to seduce him. Although both of them had hoped for more, this outburst results in the end of their relationship. Ironically, John has failed to notice that Lenina has become increasingly fond of him – '*more than anybody I've ever known*' (p. 149, ll. 17–18).

John likes Bernard because they share the experience of being outsiders. But soon the Savage realizes that Bernard is using him as an instrument to serve his own interests. When John refuses to appear at Bernard's party, he ends his friend's social success. Afterwards their friendship returns to what it was before: the closeness of two outsiders who understand each others' problems.

John's friendship with Helmholtz is deeper. They '*took to one another at once*' (p. 156, l. 14). Both are interested in literature, both long to experience real passion, and both search for words to express their feelings adequately. It is Helmholtz who helps John to interrupt the *soma* distribution because they share the conviction that *soma* prevents people from having deeper feelings, and it is Helmholtz who supports John in his discussion with Mustapha Mond.

John's disgust at the civilized world and his consequent attempt to prevent the *soma* distribution lead to his arrest and the discussion with the World Controller Mustapha Mond – the philosophical highlight of the novel (Chapters 16 and 17). John defends the values of the old world as we know it: art, religion and philosophy, sincere emotions and the rights of the individual. Their debate culminates in John's decision to reject the happiness and comfort of the World State. John makes his position clear: *'I want God, I want poetry, I want real danger, I want freedom, I want goodness. I want sin.'* (p. 206, ll. 16–17). He is aware of the negative consequences of his decision, but believes these elements nurture the development of the individual.

John realizes that he cannot be a part of the civilized world or of the Reservation. While the latter rejects him due to his otherness, he rejects the former, unable to see it from any other perspective but that of his own past (influenced by the guilt-ridden religion of the Reservation and the words of Shakespeare). This makes it also impossible for him to treat Lenina as she is: he can only conceive of her as a woman as either a whore or a heroine. The only way for him to survive is to withdraw to an uncultivated area near London. John settles in a lighthouse, trying to lead the life of a hermit and flagellating himself to atone for thoughts he considers sinful. This behaviour indicates that he too is as incapable of overcoming his upbringing as the others are of overcoming their conditioning. Eventually he becomes another form of entertainment for the masses. Overwhelmed by crowds of enthusiastic pleasure-seekers, he becomes so involved in the emotionality of the people that he ends up taking part in their sex and *soma* orgy. Feeling dirty and with no hope of living the life he wants, John commits suicide.

Revision
(what you learn about John)

- John is the naïve observer who represents someone close to the reader, as he has knowledge of religion, morality and literature.
- John reacts to much of life in the World State in the way that the average reader might.
- John is also a prisoner of his own conditioning and cannot view Lenina as she is; rather, he views her through the spectrum of his limited experience.
- John believes that suffering is good for the character.
- In the end he feels he has been made dirty by his participation in an orgy, which stands as a symbol for the inescapability of social pressure.

Key passages	Analysis
p. 100, ll. 5–23	John reveals his cultural upbringing.
p. 106, l. 1 – p. 117, l. 24	We see John's unhappy childhood though his own eyes. The feelings he experiences contrast with the lack of emotion experienced by the citizens of the World State.
p. 123, l. 28 – p. 125, l. 5	John falls in love with Lenina and describes her in words that are idealize her and therefore inappropriate.
p. 153, ll. 22–23 p. 198, l. 1 – p. 206, l. 30	John argues for a society based on feelings, even if that includes suffering.

Vocabulary: talking about John

alienated from both societies • conflict between different values • rejects the civilized world • views the world through the ideas and words of Shakespeare • eaten up by feelings of guilt • guilt-ridden • punishes himself • feels the need to atone for his sins • embodies humanitarian values / old-fashioned concepts of morality • commits suicide • acts out of despair

Mustapha Mond

Name	allusion to: • **Mustapha** Kemal Pascha, called Atatürk (1881–1938), Turkish general and politician, founder of the modern state of Turkey in 1923, in which state and religion are kept separate. • Alfred Moritz **Mond** (1868–1930), co-founder of Imperial Chemical Industries (ICI), one of the leading British chemical companies in Huxley's time; Mond tried to improve conditions for his workers.
Job	Resident Controller for Western Europe, one of the Ten World Controllers; title: *'his fordship'* (p. 31, l. 4); in his youth a *'pretty good physicist'* (p. 194, ll. 9–10).
Caste	not mentioned explicitly, but obviously an Alpha Double-Plus
Description	*'strong deep voice'* (p. 32, l. 1)

As one of the Ten World Controllers, Mustapha Mond is in charge of Western Europe and is the leading representative of the state in the novel. His function is more relevant than his individual traits, so he remains a flat character. The only thing the reader learns about him is that he has a deep voice that underlines his authority and that, as a young man, he was drawn to the search for truth through science.

Mond not only stands above the laws, but his profound knowledge and exceptional intelligence also put him above the system. That position enables him to inform the students about the development of the World State from the time of Ford up to the present. Moreover, he can discuss the philosophical principles of modern civilization with a person like John, who has a critical view of civilization due to having been brought up outside the World State. Mond's function is to introduce the reader to the very essence of the World State.

In his youth he was a good physicist, who in his search for truth overstepped the limits of what was allowed. When he was given the choice of being sent to an island and continuing pure science or of renouncing it and being taken onto the Controllers' Council, he chose the latter. It was a hard decision to give up science and serve other people's happiness, which he sees as his present duty. Having made that decision, he now upholds the World State by defending its principles, banning opponents to far-away islands, and censoring potentially dangerous books and ideas.

Nevertheless, he is still interested in scientific research and is an intelligent, open-minded person who is prepared to consider and discuss alternative views of society. Allowing John and Linda to come to London is a kind of social experiment for the Controller, which indicates that he retains his scientific curiosity. Moreover, he sympathizes with people like John and Helmholtz, who have an explorative spirit, who prefer to choose the path he did not take, who value individuality more than comfort and happiness. Ultimately, however, he will always ensure that the stability of the system remains paramount.

Mustapha Mond's private convictions often differ from the official attitude of the state. He reads prohibited books like the Bible and the works of Shakespeare and philosophers, he values art and science far beyond what the state allows its citizens, and he reflects that the purpose of life might indeed not be '*the maintenance of well-being, but some intensification and refining of consciousness, some enlargement of knowledge*' (p. 152, ll. 17–18). He even accepts that the existence of God may be possible in an irreligious world, but that God '*manifests himself as an absence*' (p. 201, l. 21). Mond is not simply a cypher for the system but is also Huxley's mouthpiece, expressing ideas that are probably also the author's. However, the contrast between Mond's personal opinions and the official doctrines, which he represents even while recognising their superficiality, even their fundamental wrongness, makes him appear cynical.

Revision
(what you learn about Mustapha Mond)

- Mond represents the system, but expresses ideas that may also be the author's.
- He is a mouthpiece for the ideas that resulted in the creation of the World State.
- While aware of the drawbacks of the system, he believes the advantages outweigh the disadvantages.

Key passages	Analysis
p. 187, l. 1 – p. 206, l. 30	Mond discusses the philosophy behind the World State.

Vocabulary: talking about Mustapha Mond

intelligent • well-read • able to hold his own in a discussion • has inside knowledge of how the system works • is not prepared to allow new ideas to be disseminated • believes in social stability • pragmatic • a realist

Lenina Crowne

Name	allusion to: • Vladimir Ilyich **Lenin** (1870–1924), Russian politician and leader of the communist October Revolution in 1917. As head of the Soviet Union he proclaimed the equality of all citizens, but shed the blood of millions of his compatriots.
Job	nurse in the Social Predestination Room of the Central London Hatchery and Conditioning Centre.
Caste	Beta

Description	*'uncommonly pretty'* (p. 17, l. 2); *'wonderfully pneumatic'* (p. 40, l. 25), i.e. sexy, perhaps with breasts that look blown up with air (= *pneuma* in Greek), comparable to silicone today; blue eyes; *'not a freemartin'* (p. 45, l. 25), which means she has to take contraceptives in order to avoid pregnancy; popular, *'had spent a night with almost all of them'* (p. 50, ll. 3–4).

Lenina is a typical product of the World State: naïve, beautiful, popular, perfectly adapted to her job and content with her life. She uses hypnopaedic slogans to express her views on life, particularly as far as her caste (*'I'm glad I'm not a Gamma'*, p. 55, l. 7; *'I'm glad I'm not an Epsilon'*, p. 64, l. 13) and her sex life are concerned (*'Everyone belongs to everyone else'*, p. 40, l. 3). The fact that she has been dating Henry Foster for four months is a cause for concern to her friend Fanny. Yet she spends her time with Henry conventionally: they fly to Obstacle Golf, then they go out dining and dancing, take *soma* and have sex.

Lenina's affair with Henry serves as a contrast to her relationships with Bernard and John, both of whom are outsiders. Lenina is interested in Bernard merely as an entertainment. Despite his physical shortcomings she finds him *'rather sweet'* (p. 42, l. 19), and their plan to go to the Reservation promises to be a thrilling experience. Their dates, however, are disappointments for both of them: Lenina wants the usual entertainment and fun, while Bernard wants to talk and let their relationship grow slowly. Lenina cannot understand his peculiar behaviour and responds to his strange comments with hypnopaedic platitudes. Finally they end up in bed together, but Bernard misses romance, while Lenina finds him *'odd, odd, odd'* (p. 75, l. 1).

Owing to their different expectations, the trip to the Reservation is a failure. Lenina is disgusted by the primitive world of the Indians, she misses the accustomed comforts of the civilized world, and she can only stand the horrible adventure with the help of *soma*.

Meeting John, however, changes her life considerably. Her character even shows signs of development. There is a strong physical attraction, and Lenina and others are curious to know *'what it's like to make love to a Savage'* (p. 143, ll. 3–4). John is different from the men in the World

State and therefore sexually appealing. Interestingly enough, it is his avoidance of intimacy that makes Lenina desire John even more; she starts to look ill and is unable to concentrate. She confesses to Fanny that *'he's the one I want'* (p. 161, l. 11), an emotion that a conditioned citizen of the World State should not really be able to experience. So her shock is therefore that much deeper when John rudely rejects her after the feely, and even hurts her when they are about to have sex.

John's brutal outburst is the end of a relationship that was doomed from the beginning because of their different concepts of love. Lenina appears at the very end of the novel as *'a young woman'* (p. 220, l. 28) who is not mentioned by name, but the reader can easily recognize her by her description and John's reaction to her presence. Although it is not clear what she wants, she has tears in her eyes and *'yearning distress'* (p. 221, l. 4), again indications that she has feelings for John which in their intensity are unusual for a person who has been conditioned their whole life to want and expect the opposite, and may be a sign of emotional development.

Revision
(what you learn about Lenina Crowne)

- As a Beta, it is much more difficult for Lenina to overcome her conditioning than it is for an Alpha.
- She is someone who enjoys sex, but deviates from the norm because her relationships are longer and, in John's case, involve rather strong feelings.
- She discovers feelings of love in herself of which she was unaware and for which she is unprepared, and she is incapable of analysing or understanding them.

Key passages	Analysis
p. 37, l. 14 – p. 38, l. 2 p. 39, ll. 28–30	Lenina fails to live according to sexual conventions: she is not very promiscuous and has only slept with one man in the previous four months.

p. 55, ll. 28–29 p. 76, l. 11 – p. 79, l. 28 p. 92, l. 12 – p. 95, l. 30	Lenina shows that in other respects she is a normal, well-conditioned young woman. She likes to be entertained in large groups, dislikes being alone, uses slogans instead of thoughts, and cannot cope with unusual experiences.
p. 149, ll. 11–30 p. 161, ll. 8–28	Lenina develops strong feelings for John.

Vocabulary: talking about Lenina Crowne

shallow • enjoys sex • object of desire • conformist idiosyncratic view of sex • dates one man for longer than is normal • develops feelings for John • triggers off John's inner conflict • is put on a pedestal by John

Helmholtz Watson

Name	allusion to: • Hermann Ludwig Ferdinand von **Helmholtz** (1821–1894), German physicist and mathematician; • John B. **Watson** (1878–1958), one of the most important American psychologists of the theory of behaviourism, which promotes learning through conditioning
Job	Emotional Engineer, composing feely scenarios and inventing slogans and hypnopaedic rhymes; lecturer at the Department of Writing at the College of Emotional Engineering
Caste	Alpha Plus
Description	'*powerfully built man … beautifully shaped head … handsome*' (p. 58, ll. 3–5)

Helmholtz Watson is portrayed as an ideal specimen of an Alpha Plus citizen: his superb intellect is matched by his handsomeness, he is a sports champion and an '*indefatigable lover*' (p. 58, l. 30), he is popular as a committee man and has lots of contacts. His superiors judge him '*able. Perhaps a little* too *able.*' (p. 58, ll. 14–16), which foreshadows future trouble. However, he has come to a point in his life at which he considers all his achievements to amount to little; he is longing for something deeper and more meaningful, yet he – a gifted writer of propagandistic texts – is unable to express what he is longing for.

Helmholtz shares his dissatisfaction with the shallow World State first with Bernard, and later with John. Although quite different from Bernard, he likes him as a friend, and feels connected to him by the common '*knowledge that they were individuals*' (p. 58, ll. 24–25). As a magnanimous person he forgives Bernard for his boasting, his self-pitying and his negligence. When Bernard breaks down emotionally in the World Controller's office, Helmholtz is the one who looks after him.

By quoting passages from Shakespeare to him, John opens a new world for the Emotional Engineer, who is fascinated by the power of Shakespeare's words. However, as a modern person he finds certain notions in Shakespeare's works incomprehensible. He bursts out laughing when John recites from *Romeo and Juliet* – Shakespeare's ideas of love and family seem too absurd to him, showing how deeply rooted he is in his society. Yet he realizes that it takes extraordinary situations to enable a poet to write extraordinary poetry.

In his efforts to overcome the limitations of experience in his world, Helmholtz risks conflict with the authorities. A poem he writes about loneliness provokes his superiors. Helmholtz spontaneously supports John in throwing *soma* out of the hospital window in a futile attempt to liberate the masses. Thereby he openly breaks the rules of society, risking banishment and the loss of everything he has achieved.

And, in fact, Helmholtz is sent to an island '*because you happen to be too much interested in beauty*' (p. 196, ll. 25–26) – the beauty of words, that is. Asked by the World Controller which island he would prefer, he requests a place with a rough climate, since he thinks that uncomfortable weather conditions encourage better writing. He is exiled to the Falkland Islands in the South Atlantic. His choice earns him the Controller's respect.

In a way, Helmholtz Watson is an almost heroic character who deserves the reader's sympathy. Although profiting from the system in nearly every regard, he gives up everything to find meaning and beauty and to further develop his individuality.

Revision
(what you learn about Helmholtz Watson)

- Helmholtz is exceptional in every sense.
- He feels that something is missing in his life, but does not know what it is.
- He is willing to give up his tranquil existence to find deeper meaning in life.

Key passages	Analysis
p. 58, ll. 3–16	Helmholtz is an impressive and successful individual
p. 58, l. 17 – p. 59, l. 5 p. 60, l. 6 – p. 61, l. 4	He feels something is missing in his life, but does not know what. He feels that he has something to say, but does not know what it is.
p. 154, l. 24 – p. 156, l. 13	When he finally writes a poem about solitude, which goes against all the beliefs of the system, Helmholtz feels as if he has said something powerful and important.
p. 158, l. 14 – p. 159, l. 13	Helmholtz realizes that Shakespeare may use powerful language, but that now it is important to find new things to write about, as Shakespeare's time was very different.

Vocabulary: talking about Helmholtz Watson

successful, talented and attractive • dissatisfied with life • searching for something deeper and more meaningful • courageous • magnanimous

Linda

Name	Ironic, as Linda means 'pretty' in Spanish
Job	Embryo-store worker
Caste	Beta-Minus
Description	old, ugly, fat, smelly, bad skin, bad teeth, alcoholic

Linda is a victim of circumstances over which she has no control. Conditioned to live in the civilized world, she is unable to cope with conditions in the Reservation when she is left behind after a visit with the D.H.C. A stranger in the world of the Indians, Linda *'had to suffer – and not a gramme of* soma *to be had'* (p. 102, ll. 29–30). Her polygamous relationships – perfectly normal according to her conditioning – lead to her being branded a whore and being hated, despised and assaulted by the Indian women. She had a lover called Popé with whom she often got drunk and had sex.

With no idea about motherhood, she did the best she could for John, telling him about 'the Other Place', singing songs to him, teaching him hypnopaedic slogans. Among the most important things John learned from her was reading and writing. However, Linda has to admit that *'there's so much one doesn't know; it wasn't my business to know'* (p. 105, ll. 1–2), which shows how little insight people have into things for which they have not been conditioned.

All in all, the time she spent in the Reservation was terrible, and she turned to alcohol, which made her situation worse.

Linda remains an outsider, even when she returns to the World State. She is rejected by the D.H.C. – her former lover – and the rest of society, as she is too ugly and decrepit, an unwanted reminder of decay and mortality, and she herself is perfectly happy to fall back into the world of *soma* and dreams. She lies in bed, *'taking holiday after holiday'* (p. 132, ll. 18–19) without regaining full consciousness before she dies in the hospital. She fails to offer John any motherly sign of love at her death, which would have allowed him to take leave of her peacefully. She remains up to the end a sexual pleasure-seeking citizen of the State.

The Director of Hatcheries and Conditioning (D.H.C.)

Name	Thomas (Tomakin as Linda calls him); no surname is given and he is referred to mostly by his position (D.H.C.)
Job	Director of the Central London Hatchery and Conditioning Centre
Caste	Alpha Plus
Description	*'tall and rather thin but upright'* (p.6, l.18)

At the beginning of the novel, the D.H.C. introduces a group of new students – and the reader – to the principles of the production and conditioning of human beings. The students follow *'the great man'* (p.6, l.2) obediently, valuing the privilege of being instructed by the Director himself. His detailed knowledge of the processes is matched by his pride in the scientific achievements of his institution.

He is a perfect servant and representative of the system, in that he never questions it. Indeed, his descriptions of the reproduction system reveal his enthusiasm, and when the World Controller takes over the talk, the D.H.C fawns over him, awed by his importance. He is a stickler for ensuring that his staff spend their free time correctly. Fanny suspects this is the reason he wants Lenina to have somebody other than Foster. Fanny is relieved to hear that the Director patted Lenina *'on the behind'*, which *'shows what* he *stands for. The strictest conventionality'* (p.38, ll.27–28).

Although suspicious of Bernard, the D.H.C. signs the travel permit for the Reservation because it comes from the Controller. In a sentimental mood, he recalls his own trip to the Reservation 25 years earlier, momentarily forgetting Bernard, who is puzzled that *'a man so conventional, so scrupulously correct as the Director'* (p.82, ll.14–15) would talk so feelingly about a personal experience in the past. As soon as he comes back to his senses, he hurriedly claims that his relation to Linda was *'nothing emotional, nothing long-drawn'* but *'perfectly healthy and normal'* (p.84, ll.2–3). Resuming the role of authority whose *'voice [...] had now become wholly righteous and impersonal – was the expression of the disapproval of Society itself*' (p. 84, ll. 16–17), he warns Bernard to change his unorthodox behaviour or be exiled to Iceland.

After Bernard's trip to the Reservation, the D.H.C. orders Bernard to the Fertilizing Room in order to make a public example of him. He accuses him of undermining stability, and hence society itself, by his scandalous attitudes towards *soma*, sex and leisure activities. When Bernard presents him with Linda and John, the Director is so humiliated that he runs out of the room and resigns from his post soon afterwards.

Unlike the World Controller Mond, who stands above the laws, the Director falls victim to his own severity where proper behaviour is concerned.

Themes

Community, Identity, Stability

The World State's motto 'Community, Identity, Stability' is not only written on the main entrance of the Central London Hatchery and Conditioning Centre, but, by being introduced in the very first paragraph of the novel, can also be interpreted as the motto of the whole novel. Although all three terms are essential to the fictional society depicted in *Brave New World*, 'stability' stands out as the ultimate goal of the World State.

Community plays a very important role in the World State. Everything people do is done in the company of others. A good example of how the feeling of community is strengthened is the regular Solidarity Service that leads to the orgiastic experience of unity.

Consequently, Bernard is regarded as 'odd' when he prefers to do things alone. This deviant behaviour fills Fanny with '*horror*' (p. 41, l. 14). Lenina, too, finds it 'funny' that Bernard blushes when they talk about their trip to the Reservation in a crowded elevator with lots of people overhearing them speaking about a plan that, in Bernard's opinion, ought to be discussed privately. Later on, she is puzzled by Bernard's '*mania [...] for doing things in private*' (p. 76, ll. 11–12), when he expresses his wish to avoid masses of people in order to be alone with her.

Like Bernard, other unorthodox characters like John and Helmholtz also avoid the masses and value solitude, because it allows them to concentrate on what they consider important. It is '*all alone, outside the pueblo, on the bare plain of the mesa*' where John '*discovered Time and Death and God*' (p. 117, ll. 11, 24). And at the end of the novel, John withdraws to the loneliness of the lighthouse to find peace, a plan which is thwarted by the arrival of curious crowds.

What the outcasts try to find in solitude is exactly what the World State does not want people to seek: the opportunity to discover one's individuality, to question one's own values and those of society.

Community is also what people work for and what gives purpose to their work. Work is what gives cohesion to society, even if it is often pointless, as can be seen from the experiment in Ireland (p.193, ll.2–24). Everyone is seen as being useful for a successful society. The usefulness of the individual is stressed even after death: Henry Foster rejoices in the thought that it is '*fine to think we can go on being socially useful even after we're dead*' (p.63, ll.16–17) due to phosphorus recovery.

Identity in the World State can be interpreted in several ways. First there is the physical identity of Bokanovsky's process, which produces up to 96 identical twins of the lower castes. Whereas the D.H.C. celebrates this form of identity as proof of 'progress', it is precisely this sameness that makes John vomit: he compares the numerous twins to '*maggots*' (p.180, l.22).

The belief in the equality of man that arose during the Enlightenment can now only be found in the physico-chemical equality of people following their death, with each contributing the same amount of phosphorus.

As well as there being so many people (the Gammas, Deltas and Epsilons) who are physically identical, almost everybody's life is identical. This applies to the way people are produced and educated, to their interests and forms of entertainment, to their lifestyles in general, even to their treatment after death. People do not change physically during their lives as the process of ageing has been overcome, and their '*characters remain constant throughout a whole lifetime*' (p.48, ll.21–22). These similarities are mirrored in names: only 10,000 different names are used by 2 billion people.

Moreover, identity is also a factor in the relationship between citizen and state. The 'individual' completely identifies with the World State, which provides him or her with everything, and for whose well-being everyone works. Henry Foster demonstrates this attitude when he talks about technological progress '*as though it had been his own*' (p. 63, l.16).

What is true for the citizens is also true for society as a whole: it has stopped changing due to the reforms following the Nine Years' War and, according to the intention of the rulers, will remain unchanged forever, thus guaranteeing stability.

Stability is the highest value in the World State, '*the primal and the ultimate need*' (p.39, ll.23–24), to which every other aspect is subordinate. The stability of the individual is the precondition of the stability of the state. So, in his lecture to the students, World Controller Mustapha Mond proclaims that there is *'no civilization without social stability. No social stability without individual stability'* (p. 39, ll. 2–3), or in the words of a hypnopaedic slogan *'When the individual feels, the community reels'* (p. 80, l. 30).

The stability of the individual citizen is achieved by a state of permanent happiness, stability *'in contentment'* (p. 39, l. 13). If personal problems occur, *soma* helps the individual become happy and calm again. Factors that caused instability in the past have been eliminated – emotions between lovers and family members, but also diseases and poverty. Likewise, high art, pure science and religion have had to be sacrificed for the sake of social stability. It is accepted that the *'iceberg'* society (p. 192, l. 27), in which one-ninth is above the water line (the Alphas and Betas) and eight-ninths are below (the lower castes), provides the greatest stability.

The result of this radical transformation of society is *'the stablest equilibrium in history'* (p. 195, ll. 29–30). As the banishment of Helmholtz and Bernard and the suicide of John prove, every attempt to bring about a change is doomed to failure. History (in the sense of a historical development) has come to an end, since relevant development no longer takes place.

Points to remember

- The World State lays most of its emphasis on stability, as it insists that real happiness can only exist in a stable society.
- Identity is unchangeable: once one has been formed as an individual, one retains that identity throughout life.
- The individual only has relevance as a member of the community.

History

One of the greatest 'achievements' of the regime is the elimination of any historical consciousness. *'History is bunk'*, and so people are no longer taught history.

The turning point in history was the Nine Years' War starting in A.F. 141. Life before was characterized by instability due to strong feelings in personal relationships, particularly among family members. Home meant *'darkness, disease, and smells'* (p. 34, ll. 7–8). Movements to improve misery – Christianity, liberalism and democracy – failed because, according to Mond, they were based on a misunderstanding of what human beings really are and what they need. The Savage Reservation in New Mexico, admission to which is strictly limited, has been retained as a reminder of the past. Huxley describes all the repulsive aspects of life that Bernard and Lenina encounter there, such as dirt, poverty, superstition.

The Nine Years' War signalled the end of civilization as we know it. The war was fought with chemical and biological weapons and was followed by a great 'Economic Collapse'. What Mond says about this war reminds one of World War I (1914–1918), while the 'Economic Collapse' reminds one of the World Economic Crisis which started in 1929 on 'Black Friday', when the collapse of the New York Stock Exchange drove millions into ruin.

The war left only the *'choice between World Control and destruction'* (p. 44, ll. 8–9). People were willing to give up *'anything for a quiet life'* (p. 196, l. 21). In a short period of transition, governments tried to stabilize society by ordering a certain level of consumption in order to keep production going. However, a lot of people reacted by withdrawing into nature or culture, thereby consuming almost nothing. Soon the governments realized that there was no use in enforcing a mode of behaviour, so they took to the *'infinitely surer methods of ectogenesis, neo-Pavlovian conditioning and hypnopaedia'* (p. 45, ll. 22–23). In a *'campaign against the Past'* (p. 46, l. 5) museums were closed, historical monuments (like the pyramids) were destroyed and books (e.g. those of Shakespeare) were suppressed. Christianity, which propagated *'the philosophy of under-consumption'* (p. 46, l. 23), was replaced by Community Sings, Solidarity Services and the adoration of the arch-Capitalist Ford. The invention of *soma*, the perfect drug with no side-effects, made alcohol and conventional drugs redundant. The last thing that had to be overcome to create a happy world was old age. Although the Controller, in his discussion with John, deplores some aspects of the development – the sacrifice of art and independent science in particular – he defends them for the sake of the highest good in the World State: universal happiness.

Mustapha Mond mentions history to the students only to make them fully aware of the enormous achievements of modern civilization, but in everyday life history does not play a role. All that people know is the present, and the present is all people need to know in order to be happy. A knowledge of the past may make one nostalgic, or lead one to consider alternative societal forms, both of which could lead to unhappiness: *'Was and will make me ill. I take a gramme and only am'* (p. 89, ll.31–32). Historical knowledge is restricted to the elite of the World Controllers, as Mond reveals in his discussions in Chapters 16 and 17. Even the personal reminiscences of the past by the D.H.C. about his trip to the Reservation are considered to be embarrassing and unconventional.

Points to remember

- It took extreme conflict and suffering before people finally chose to live in a stable society which abolished the past.
- Citizens of the state are discouraged from looking back into the past, so even memories are discouraged.

Happiness

The major premise of the novel is the idea that happiness is the quality that most people seek. In order to achieve happiness for everyone the World State has had to change people and society dramatically.

Soma

Soma is the most important way in which people avoid unhappiness or sadness. *Soma* both calms people and makes them high, yet it has no side effects. Mond sums up the benefits of soma in this way: *'And if ever, by some unlucky chance, anything unpleasant should somehow happen, why, there's always* soma *to give you a holiday from the facts. And there's always* soma *to calm your anger, to reconcile you to your enemies, to make you patient and long-suffering. In the past you could only accomplish these things by making a great effort and after years of hard moral training. Now, you swallow two or three half-gramme tablets, and there you are. Anybody can be virtuous now. You can carry at least half your morality about in a bottle. Christianity without tears – that's what* soma *is.'* (p.204, ll.22–31). *Soma* allows citizens of the World State to avoid the unpleasant truths of their existence, which people in other societies had to deal with. The confrontation with these truths may have helped or harmed the individual. Now no one needs to worry about these truths. Indeed, *soma* seems to have taken the place of religion to such an extent that the pseudo-religious Solidarity Service centres around a communion service in which a cup of *soma* is passed around, just like the cup of wine is passed around in a Christian service. *Soma* makes the need for suffering, God and complex feeling unnecessary.

Relationships

Human relationships have fundamentally changed in the World State. Deep emotions, be they positive or negative, have been largely eliminated from relationships, as they are seen to have been the major source of personal and therefore social instability in the past.

Ectogenesis (i.e. birth outside the womb) in the Hatchery Centre has replaced natural birth, thereby removing the natural bond between mother and child. As is the case with any unusual practice connected with sex and reproduction, terms like 'mother' and 'father' become first redundant and then taboo. How embarrassing and humiliating the use of such words has become can be seen from the reaction of the Hatchery staff to John addressing the D.H.C. as his father. Abolishing parents also resulted in the end of family life. In his talk to the students, Mustapha Mond derides the family home as being characterized by '*darkness, disease, and smells*' (p. 34, ll. 7–8). Mothers are made to resemble animals '*periodically teeming*' and '*brooding*' over their children '*like a cat over its kittens*' (p. 34, ll. 6, 25). Mond refers to Sigmund Freud, whom he quotes as '*the first to reveal the appalling dangers of family life*' (p. 36, ll. 1–2) leading to misery, perversion, madness and suicide. Children are brought up in Conditioning Centres with no parents.

In later life, adults are encouraged to have sex with everyone, thereby diminishing the feelings of one person for another. Sex is a pleasurable experience, and generally makes people happy. The World State therefore emphasizes sex as a way of getting people to feel pleasure as often as possible. By encouraging people to have sex with everyone, romance and love have been destroyed. In the World State '*everyone belongs to everyone else*' (p. 40, l. 3), so relationships have been more or less reduced to a sexual basis. Feelings used to cause emotional pressure in the *'poor pre-moderns'* (p.38, l.12) which the Controller compares to *'water under pressure in a pipe'* (p.38, l.3). As they only had a single outlet for their emotions, their feelings were very strong, causing instability on a personal and social level. In Mond's view, modern civilization has reduced the pressure, thereby allowing people to be *'sane, virtuous, happy'* (p.38, 14). When sex is denied, other feelings emerge. Thus we see Lenina *'with a strange feeling of anxious exultation'* (p.149, l.14) when she is waiting to see John after he refused to have sex with her. Her frustration can only be relieved by having sex with John, or by transforming these feelings into infatuation and then into love, which is exactly what the World State wants to avoid.

As promiscuity has become normality, Fanny is really worried about the fact that Lenina has been dating Henry Foster for about four months – she recommends a Pregnancy Substitute treatment to Lenina. When Lenina talks to Bernard in the elevator about their trip to the Reservation, she *'publicly proved her unfaithfulness to Henry Foster'* (p.50, ll.21–22), thus demonstrating that her behaviour is healthy and normal. As she is a popular girl, she *'had spent a night with almost all'* (p.50, ll.3–4) of the men in the lift. Similarly, the D.H.C. emphasizes that his relationship to Linda in the Reservation was *'nothing emotional. Nothing long-drawn. It was all perfectly healthy and normal'* (p.84, ll.2–3).

However, there are also men who are not satisfied with this sort of sex and the shallowness of emotions in a conventional relationship: Helmholtz, Bernard and John. Helmholtz, the 'indefatigable lover' who is said to have had *'six hundred and forty different girls in under four years'* (p.58, ll.30–31), is no longer as happy as he should be and longs for something more. What he is interested in, however, is not a real and meaningful relationship, but rather the need to express something important which he feels inside.

When we meet Bernard, he is seeking some sort of romance with Lenina. He wants to talk, to *'try the effect of arresting my impulses [...] to know what passion is [...] to feel something strongly'* (p.80, ll.1, 28–29), and he would prefer to wait before they sleep together. Even though it turns out later in the novel that his attitude to promiscuity has been shaped by his lack of opportunity, and even if he enjoys having any woman he likes during his period of success, he does seem to feel that the lack of emotion in merely sexual relationships is a bad thing.

As in other respects, too, John has a diametrically opposed notion of human relationships from the citizens of the World State. Being used to family life in the Reservation – however depressing it may have been sometimes – he loves his mother Linda, wants her to accompany him on his trip to civilization, and he cares for her when she is dying as a result of *soma* abuse.

In his relationship with Lenina, John has been shaped by Indian traditions and Shakespearean ideals. He really loves Lenina, and identifies with Romeo's love for Juliet. But before he would be willing to marry or sleep with her, he wants to prove himself '*worthy*' (p.163, l.4) by doing something heroic.

Marriage in the Reservation means being married to one partner for the rest of one's life. However, when he talks about marriage, Lenina is '*genuinely shocked*' (p.164, l.19) by the idea of staying with only one man for ever. By confessing his love to the girl, he encourages her to seduce him, but her behaviour, which would be absolutely normal in a relationship with any other man, inspires a violent reaction on his part, terminating their relationship.

John and Lenina's relationship has to fail because of the vast gulf between their upbringings and thinking concerning love and sex. John's mother experiences something equally devastating in the traditional society of the Reservation: her promiscuity, the only pattern for relationships she knows, causes her to be treated as a whore by the men who take advantage of her attitude, and abused by their wives.

Culture

High culture has been eliminated (at times brutally, as can be seen in Chapter Three,). In the discussion in Chapters 16 and 17, Mond argues that there is no need for high culture in a society in which everyone is happy: '*You've got to choose between happiness and what people used to call high art*' (p.190, ll.8–9). If people live in a state of perpetual happiness, they will be incapable of understanding the demands high culture puts on them. The emotions and passions and depths of Shakespeare's plays cannot be understood by people living for superficial stimulation.

Instead of high culture, people are offered mindless entertainment, and are encouraged to participate in mass entertainment events like sport and the feelies in order to avoid truly intimate contact with others. The feelies offer mindless pornographic stories in which the feeling of a bearskin rug leaves more of an impression than the (admittedly non-existent) emotions of the characters in the feely. Alternatively there are cabarets where one can blissfully dance the night away with hundreds of others.

All these entertainments stress the sensual, fun side of life. There are no forms of entertainment that stimulate the intellect.

Work

People are produced to fulfil a particular function or work within society, so that everyone is happy with their status. It is never clear exactly how the World State works on an economic basis, except to fulfil consumerism, but even this seems to involve too much state control. The only jobs with which the reader is presented are those related to producing and conditioning people, and creating propaganda to keep people happy. The lower castes work in menial jobs in factories. But everyone is happy within their status. People have been hypnopaedically conditioned not to want more with slogans like *'Alpha children [...] work much harder than we do, because they're so frightfully clever. I'm really awfully glad I'm a Beta, because I don't work so hard.'* (p. 26, ll. 22–24). But there is the suggestion that work is meaningless. Even the Alphas do not seem to be convinced that there is meaning in their work, except as a way of passing time. Mond states quite clearly that work is just another form of happiness: it keeps people occupied and therefore happy; *'it would be sheer cruelty to afflict them with excessive leisure'* (p. 193, ll. 14–15).

Death

Death is one of the most unpleasant facts of life. Nobody really wants to die, and people often turn to religion when confronted with death as a way of coming to terms with it: *'it is the fear of death and of what comes after death that makes men turn to religion'* (p. 200, ll. 14–15). In order to prevent the unhappiness associated with death and it approach, the World State has eliminated the visible signs of old age, so people are unaware that they are approaching death. The State also tries to eliminate feelings of loss and sadness connected with death by conditioning children to associate simple pleasures like chocolate éclairs with death. This undermines any feelings of mourning or spiritual depth.

Points to remember

- The World State has been set up to provide happiness for everyone.
- Happiness involves avoiding or ignoring unpleasant aspects of life, not feeling any deep emotions, and not reflecting on one's situation.
- In such a society culture is no longer necessary or relevant, and only sensual pleasurable entertainment is needed.

Formal Aspects

Structure

Brave New World consists of 18 chapters, which can be divided into three major parts. The setting is London (parts one and three) and the Reservation (part two) in the year A.F. (After Ford) 632.

introduction to the World State	1–3	Nature of the state
	3	Introduction of the characters
	4–6.ii	Insight into the life of the characters
reservation	6.iii–9	Life on the Reservation
John in the World State	10–15	John's reaction to the World State
	16–17	Discussion of the World State
	18	Withdrawal and death of John

In the first six chapters the reader is introduced to the principles and living conditions of the World State. Important characters (Bernard, Lenina, Mond) are introduced in this section. The first three chapters, which can be called the exposition, are a rather static description of the new world, and the actual plot starts in Chapter 4, which focuses on the protagonist of this section, Bernard Marx, his role in society, his relationship with Lenina, and the preparations for their joint trip to the Reservation.

The second part (Chapter 6, Part 3 – Chapter 9) is about Bernard's and Lenina's experiences in the Reservation. This section serves several purposes: to contrast the civilized and the primitive worlds, and to introduce John as another protagonist, who becomes the pivotal character of the plot after the return to London.

The third main part (Chapters 10–18) deals with John's confrontation with the civilized world. First, the reactions of John and the citizens of the World State to each other are dealt with (Chapters 10–15): John is appalled by most aspects of the civilized world, whereas its citizens are superficially fascinated by his otherness and novelty value. Furthermore, the focus shifts from Bernard's futile relationship with Lenina to John's love for her. The scandal during *soma* distribution in the hospital leads to the philosophical discussion of the fundamental ideas on which the new society has been erected (Chapters 16 and 17).

Huxley has constructed some parallel scenes in the novel in order to elicit comparisons and to contrast characters and ideas.

The first use of parallelism comes at the end of the Chapter Three, where different voices are heard. Here, for example, Lenina's and Fanny's trivial conversation about clothes (pp. 45–47) is contrasted with the Controller's description of the establishment of the new society and the eradication of the culture of the past; the Controller's description of past emotions and passions is undermined by Bernard's feelings of anger at Henry and his desire for Lenina (p. 42).

Other examples of parallelism are:

a) How different characters spend an evening with Lenina:
   - Henry Foster, who does so in a conventional way (Chapter 4, Part 1, and Chapter 5, Part 1);
   - Bernard, who tries to cling to his individuality, but finally gives in to soma and sex (Chapter 6, Part 1);
   - John, who rigidly resists Lenina's attempts to seduce him (Chapter 13).

b) Another example is the description of religious rites. The Solidarity Service with its superficial religious elements (Chapter 5, Part 2) contrasts with the serious, unpleasant and bloody ceremony of the Indians (Chapter 7), but also with John's experience of God in the solitude of the plains (p. 117)

Points to remember

- The novel can be divided largely into 3 parts.
- The first chapters serve as an introduction to the workings of the World State.

Narration

Brave New World is narrated by an omniscient narrator. While the narrator is by and large objective throughout the novel, the perspective does change slightly. Even in Chapter One, with its long scientific descriptions, there is an ironic distance between the narrator and the material. Sentences like *'Straight from the horse's mouth into the notebook'* (p.6, ll.16–17) and *'The pencils were busy'* (p.8, l.7) indicate that he is also making fun of the diligence of the students, who are learning about inhuman processes.

In the following chapters, the perspective is mostly Bernard Marx's. Unlike the other characters, Bernard's thoughts are conveyed to the reader directly (cf. p.42, ll.5–9 and Part Two of Chapter Four). It would be difficult to show the perspective of the other characters of the World State as they are happy within their environment, and total contentment is not a productive or engaging perspective from which to narrate. Moreover, by showing us the thoughts of one character who does not seem at home in the utopian society, Huxley offers an outsider's perspective for the reader to identify with.

However, when John makes his appearance in Chapter Seven, the perspective changes. In Chapter Eight we see the story of his life. Although we assume that this story is the one he is telling Bernard and Lenina, the story is presented as a series of fragmented third-person narratives, which probably reflect his real memories. We find ourselves immersed in John's experiences and understand the pain he has gone through as he grew up. These experiences are unusual, as none of the characters in the World State have experienced such sadness and loneliness. This particular narrative perspective stands outside the mainstream narrative, offering us the memories of a character. None of the other characters have a real past with interesting memories.

The author allows the reader a new perspective on the World State by introducing John, as he is closer in many ways to our society than the other characters in the novel (even those like Helmholtz and Bernard who are both discontented with society). John watches what goes on, learns, and reflects on what he sees. Yet, as with Bernard earlier, the reader learns to detach him- or herself from John as a figure of identification. As John becomes increasingly estranged from the

World State, his actions and beliefs become increasingly bizarre. His exaggerated self-torture arising from the mixture of erotic and emotional reactions to Lenina, which lead to isolation and self-flagellation, does not endear him to the reader. If love with Lenina is impossible due to her conditioning, so too is John's love unreasonable. It seems that the idea of needing to suffer for love is more important than love itself. It is noticeable that the epithet used for John – 'the Savage' – becomes more common as the novel proceeds. When he is introduced, he is referred to as John or 'the young man'. In the final chapter, he is merely 'the Savage'.

Huxley uses narration to distance us from the characters. While we gain insight into their thoughts, much of what they think is treated with irony. In Chapter Two, Section 1, Lenina's thoughts allow the reader to see the mindset of a typical citizen of the World State, but at the same time, they are amusing (e.g. her reflection on her public unfaithfulness on p. 50, ll. 21–23). Occasionally, the author allows the direct thoughts of society in general: *'Finally – and this was by far the strongest reason for people's not wanting to see poor Linda – there was her appearance. Fat: having lost her youth; with bad teeth, and a blotched complexion, and that figure (Ford!) – you simply couldn't look at her without feeling sick, yes, positively sick'* (p. 132, ll. 11–15). Within two sentences the author has moved from authorial intrusion ('poor') to revealing the direct thoughts of the citizens.

Far more important for Huxley and his novel are not the characters, but the ideas. The characters merely serve as mouthpieces or instruments to express the ideas in the novel. Huxley's intention is to show that a perfect society cannot exist without losing something. The ancient world of the Reservation with its wild and primitive moral values (represented by John) is not a feasible alternative to the World State. What Huxley wants to show is that humanity's future should lie somewhere between a failed past with nonsensical beliefs, and an inhuman super-future in which the problems of humanity have been solved but at an extremely high price.

Points to remember

- The omniscient narrator changes perspective quite often, starting off with a perspective that is largely Bernard's before shifting to John's perspective.
- We are often given the direct thoughts of other characters (e.g. Lenina) and of the general thoughts of the citizens.
- In Chapter 8 we are shown John's fragmented memories.
- The author uses the narrator to maintain an ironical distance to the characters.

Satire

While *Brave New World* was begun as a parody of a utopian novel by H.G. Wells (cf. p.92), it ended as a satire on the kind of progressive thinking that was sweeping through Europe and North America at the time. At the beginning of the 20th century, the human character was increasingly understood as being the creation of external forces, which could be manipulated. Huxley takes this idea to an extreme by showing human beings as the product of mass production, which had been introduced on a large scale by Henry Ford, and of conditioning.

The fact that Huxley gives his characters the names of supposedly progressive political and scientific thinkers of his time is an indication that he wants to portray a dystopian world in which their ideas have been realized – but in an extreme form. Huxley's technique is to extrapolate current developments into the future.

The same is true for other aspects of modern societies: the advertising industry, which reduces people to homogenized target groups, and the entertainment industries, which provide simplistic entertainment for the masses. Huxley was worried that he was living in an age in which individuality was being reduced and in which people were becoming dehumanized. Of course, society today is very different. The end of totalitarianism in Europe and the lessons learned from the inhuman practices of the Nazis has made it almost impossible to promote one particular form of society in which people fit like pegs. The pill and other forms of contraception have liberalized sexuality; drugs are more readily available and have also been proven to be not only incapable of creating permanent states of happiness, but to be destructive and dangerous; mass entertainment is an integral part of our lives (yet high art continues to exist); *in vitro* fertilization has become a normal process. From a modern perspective, not all the developments depicted in *Brave New World* are as horrific as they would have seemed to Huxley. Huxley's prophecies seem to have been realized in some areas, e.g. cloning, the consumerist mentality, the weakening of family ties.

Yet Huxley, as a progressive modern man, is not so foolish as to wish to halt the progress that is taking place. He merely wishes to point out where it might lead. Indeed, he prevents critics from urging a return to old values by satirizing centuries-old belief systems. In his depiction of the Reservation he satirizes the use of bloody appeals for aid to the gods. By mixing in old Indian and Christian elements he

Indios in a traditional prayer ritual

manages to distance the reader from the religious cultic ceremony shown in Chapter Seven, when a man is whipped in order '*to make the rain come and the corn grow*' (p. 100, ll. 19–20). The apparent hypocrisy of sexual-moral values in the pre-Modern world, exemplified by the Pueblo, is shown by the fact that extramarital sex is discouraged, while the men are happy to indulge in it. The unfairness of life in primitive societies is seen in the treatment of John, who is isolated because of his mixed blood and because his mother is treated as a whore. Indeed, John – a product of this primitive culture – at the end becomes a hermit, flagellating himself because he has found no proper outlet for his desire for Lenina.

Huxley forces the reader to consider his or her own moral values by holding up two societies – one, the civilized future in which humans have been dehumanized and stripped of the capacity for deep thoughts or feelings, and the other, a primitive society relying on nonsensical religious ideas for its survival.

Points to remember

- Huxley is satirizing the modern trends in his society, which seemed to offer humans a cure for their individual problems and for the social ills around them.
- By only offering two extreme and unpleasant forms of society, Huxley forces the reader to consider his or her own moral values.

Background

Utopian Literature

The dream of a better world is as old as human consciousness. Threatened by hunger, illness, danger, inexplicable natural catastrophes and the brutal dominance of the strong, early human beings invented stories, normally embedded in a religious context, about an existence without needs and fears. The following survey is restricted to important milestones of utopian literature and to those works that Aldous Huxley, as an educated author, will have read and which may have influenced *Brave New World*.

The first written document of an early oral tradition of utopian stories in our culture is the tale of the Garden of Eden in the Bible (Book of Genesis). An interesting ironic contrast between the two stories is that whereas curiosity leads Adam and Eve to lose the innocence of paradise, Huxley allows the inhabitants of the World State in *Brave New World* to return to a state of permanent happiness at the price of giving up any critical attitude and curiosity.

In his dialogue *Politeia (The Republic)*, the Greek philosopher Plato (ca 428–348 BC) was the first to develop a sophisticated plan for an ideal state. Characteristic elements of the society described in *Brave New World* can be found in Plato's book, e.g. the concept that an ideal state can only be stable if its citizens are socially and mentally stable. All people are assigned, according to their abilities, to castes (producers, warriors, guardians) that are responsible for certain functions within the state. In order to achieve the ideal state, Plato suggested the use of eugenics, by choosing partners for reproduction and by abandoning disabled children. Plato suggested the abolition of the family as an institution in favour of communities which possess everything in common (including women and children). This would encourage the citizens to focus on the community, thereby preventing any form of individual selfishness and dynastic thinking. A by-product of this would also be more sexual liberty.

There are two major utopian works in Latin literature: Cicero's (106-43 BC) *De re publica (On the Republic)*, which in a time of political crisis recommends a return to the old ideals of the Roman republic as the only ideal state that has been realized in history; and *De civitate Dei (The City of God)* by the Church teacher Augustine of Hippo (354–430), who shifts the focus of the ideal community from this world to the divine sphere.

It was not until the Renaissance that social and intellectual developments revived the quest for alternatives to contemporary states of world government. These developments included:

- the gradual decay of the static medieval world with the dominance of the Church and its insistence on eternal life over earthly life;
- the rekindled interest in the ideas of Antiquity during the Renaissance, which was promoted by contacts with the Arabs in Spain and the fall of Constantinople in 1456, when Greek scholars moved to western Europe;
- the discovery and exploration of new countries and continents (e.g. Columbus's arrival in America in 1492), which made people curious about alien civilizations.

The island of Utopia from Thomas More's book.

The most prominent utopian author of the Renaissance was Thomas More (1478–1535), who offered a criticism of contemporary social and political life together with his dream of a better world in the form of a travel report to the fictitious island of 'Utopia'. However, the reader quickly discovers that the allegedly ideal state is not as ideal as the narrator wants him to believe. The name 'utopia' derives from the Greek words *ou* ('not') and *topos* ('place'), meaning 'no-place land'. It also contains a pun, however, because in English 'utopia' sounds like *eutopia*, ('good-place land'), as the Greek prefix *eu* means 'good'. Later, his book gave its name to the genre. Other important utopian works of the Renaissance are Roger Bacon's *The New Atlantis* and Tommaso Campanella's *The City of the Sun*.

The rapid upheavals of the Industrial Revolution in the 19th century caused utopian literature to develop in different directions: science fiction, political writings, and dystopias (negative utopias).

Many 19th-century writers were fascinated by the new possibilities brought about by the unprecedented explosion of scientific discoveries and technological inventions, and created utopian novels whose more or less conventional plots were set in a distant world full of new and fantastic technologies. Prominent examples of science fiction of the time are the adventure novels of Jules Verne (1828–1905), who wrote of travelling to the moon and underwater journeys, Mary Shelley's *Frankenstein* (1818), and H.G. Wells's *The Time Machine* (1895).

Political writings tended to concentrate on the fact that scientific progress was not always accompanied by social progress. On the contrary, in the first decades of the Industrial Revolution, workers often lived in worse conditions than farmers and craftsmen in pre-industrial times, which inspired a large number of political writings urging the improvement of workers' living conditions. Karl Marx's influential *The Capital* (1867) became the 'bible' of socialism and communism. His principal demand was for equality in society, in order to end the conflict between the bourgeoisie and working classes. Marx's ideas influenced many politicians in the 20th century, but as can be seen by the dictatorships that emerged in Russia under Lenin and China under Mao, his ideas could never be realized. Both Marx and Lenin are referred to in the names of people in *Brave New World* (Bernard Marx and Lenina Crowne) to emphasize that the old communist ideal of general equality had been achieved in quite a surprising way.

Before *Brave New World*, most descriptions of future societies tended to be optimistic utopias. In contrast to them, *The Time Machine* (1895) by H.G. Wells, one of the most prominent British writers of the time, is a shocking extrapolation of the social injustice of his time. However, Wells tended to have an optimistic view of the future as can be seen in his works like *A Modern Utopian* (1905) and *Men like Gods* (1923). Indeed, Huxley was moved by *Men Like Gods* to write a parody of it, which then became *Brave New World*. Yevgeny Zamyatin's novel *We*, completed ten years before in 1920, has been suggested as an influence because its plot shows a lot of remarkable parallels to *Brave New World*, but Huxley stated that he had not known of the book at the time.

Wells and Huxley were the first successful authors of dystopias. Dystopian (from Greek *dys* – 'bad', hence 'bad-place land') literature takes from science fiction the setting of a world that technology has made different from our own world, and from socialism a deep dissatisfaction that no discovery or invention can lead to a perfect world. Usually writers of dystopian literature employ a future world to criticize the present one, and to issue warnings as to where current trends and developments might lead. The post-War period of the 20th century saw some outstanding depictions of dystopian societies. Amongst them are George Orwell's *1984* (1948), which describes a socialist dictatorship based on war and propaganda, Ray Bradbury's *Fahrenheit 451* (1953), and Margaret Atwood's *The Handmaid's Tale* (1985), which describes a religious dictatorship in a world in which women exist to procreate or serve men.

Points to remember

- There is a long tradition of utopian literature, which reflects a human desire for a better life.
- In the 20th century writers started to concentrate on the negative aspects of possible future societies.
- All utopias are based on trends evident in the author's own society.

Brave New World and Shakespeare

William Shakespeare (1564–1616) is still widely considered the greatest poet and playwright of the English language. His work comprises tragedies (e.g. *Romeo and Juliet, Macbeth, Othello*), comedies (e.g. *A Midsummer Night's Dream, Much Ado about Nothing, The Taming of the Shrew*), history plays (e.g. *Richard III*) and poems (sonnets, long poems).

In *Brave New World* Huxley uses Shakespeare as an example of the old culture that has been swept away by the new society. When John was about twelve, his mother's lover Popé gave him *The Complete Works of William Shakespeare*. Although Linda thinks it seems '*to be full of nonsense*' (p. 112, ll. 27–28), she keeps it for John to practice reading. Not only does John read it, he learns many passages by heart. As it is the only book he owns, he takes refuge in it when he feels bad. This allows John to use Shakespeare quotations to examine the difference between the two societies.

The most prominent quotation from Shakespeare is the title of the novel. 'Brave New World' is taken from *The Tempest*, in which Prospero and his daughter Miranda have been cast upon a lonely island. After twelve years, the magician Prospero causes the ship of his brother (and rival) to be wrecked on his island. For the first time in her life Miranda sees human beings other than her father and their deformed servant Caliban. The sight overwhelms the young woman and she exclaims:

O wonder!
How many goodly (i.e. attractive) *creatures are there here!*
How beauteous (i.e. beautiful) *mankind is! O brave* (i.e. beautiful) *new world*
that has such people in it!
(*The Tempest*, V, 1, 182ff.)

Like Miranda, John has been told about civilization and its people, but has never seen it or them with his own eyes, so their cleanliness and Lenina's beauty captivate him from the very first moment. Lenina and the prospect of accompanying Bernard and Lenina to 'the Other Place' remind John of Miranda's situation and emotions. His utterance of the words 'brave new world' is joyful. But the reader is aware of the irony, as he or she knows the 'brave new world' is full of horrors. Indeed the next time these words are quoted by John his tone has changed to ironic. Faced with the multitude of identical batches of workers at the factory, John repeats the words 'brave new world', but this time in disgust. Later he repeats them when he is confronted by the Deltas at the hospital. Here, the words at first seem derisive and cynical, but then they '*change their tone*' (p. 181, ll. 23–24), calling him to transform the nightmare into something that can be justly named a 'brave new world'. John decides to liberate the Deltas and throw away their *soma*.

The most important Shakespearean dramas within the novel are *Romeo and Juliet* and *Othello*. It seems almost self-evident that John uses lines from Shakespeare's tragedy about love to describe Lenina's beauty and his feelings towards her. There are parallels between Romeo and Juliet, whose love is doomed by the enmity between their families, and John and Lenina, whose different upbringings prevent the fulfilment of their love. However, for John his image of Lenina as a Juliet-like lover seems more important than who Lenina really is (*'for all the time he was seeing himself as Romeo and Lenina as Juliet*', p. 157, ll. 23–24). So, instead of meeting Lenina and others at Bernard's party, John withdraws to read *'with rapture*' (p. 152, l. 24) Juliet's description.

Romeo and Juliet

Othello, based on the violence that follows jealousy of one's lover, forms a contrast to the feely *Three Weeks in a Helicopter* which John and Lenina attend. The feely represents popular culture in the World State with a simple plot (perhaps a comment on the lack of depth of the movies of Huxley's time) that allows full use of the potential of modern entertainment technology. Unlike Lenina, who is enthusiastic about the feely, John is horrified by the pornographic action. As soon as he retires to his room, he takes out *Othello* because the protagonist of the movie was a black man like the Shakespearean character.

In John's discussion with the World Controller about the value of art, both agree that *Othello* is a masterpiece. But whereas John wants people to become acquainted with such beautiful works of literature, their very beauty is the reason Mond forbids them: nobody is allowed to be attracted by old things which contain beauty and deep feeling. Besides, plays like *Othello* require a world like Shakespeare's, in which emotions form the basis of real drama (Othello kills his wife Desdemona, whom he loves dearly, out of blind jealousy; Romeo and

Juliet die because they cannot be together). Emotions lead to instability, hence high art has had to be sacrificed for universal happiness in the World State.

While Shakespeare's art and values may represent the opposite of the values of the World State, nevertheless in John's usage Shakespeare's words often seem to be misplaced. His descriptions of Lenina, using words from *Romeo and Juliet* such as *'steal immortal blessing from her lips'*, *'vestal modesty'* and *'thinking their own kisses sin'* (p. 124, ll. 17–19) are inappropriate for a 'civilized' woman, for whom there is no such thing as 'stealing' kisses, the concept of virginity as a virtue, or even sin. He cannot accept the fact that Lenina is sensual, promiscuous and sexually active. Later on, he refers to her as an *'impudent strumpet'* (p. 167, l. 8), which is what Othello calls his wife, whom he will later murder. John's use of Shakespearean quotations is not dissimilar from the World State's use of slogans: these are not original words, but are instead memorized phrases which the lazy mind can easily fall back onto. This is evident in his attempt to speak to the Deltas at the hospital. The first thing he says is *'Lend me your ears'* (p. 182, ll. 16–17) – the start of the most famous speech (from *Julius Caesar)* before a crowd in literature. John, however, cannot think of what to say, and then fails to make an eloquent speech.

Shakespeare's influence on John is not restricted to words, but goes much further. John adopts 16th-century values that seem out of place in the new world. Sometimes, even his actions are inspired by characters from the old dramas. For example, as a boy, John suffered due to Popé dominating his mother's attentions. Although he only partly understands Hamlet's hate-filled words about his criminal stepfather, John feels their power, and uses them to express his hatred of Popé, making it more real. *'Like drums'* (p. 113, l. 22) Shakespeare's words repeat themselves in his head until he is finally driven to stab Popé. Later with Lenina, John does not seem aware that his words reflect dangerous passions associated with violence and death.

Helmholtz Watson is also able to value the beauty of Shakespeare's language. As an Emotional Engineer he lectures students on the power of words to influence, through slogans or feely scripts. Yet he feels that there must be something beyond what he has done so far. When John introduces him to Shakespeare's words, Helmholtz immediately senses their power, and *'trembled with an unprecedented emotion'* (p. 157, ll. 4–5). He acknowledges that Shakespeare's ability would make *'our best propaganda technicians look silly'* (p. 157, ll. 31f.). Nevertheless, even he bursts out laughing when Juliet pathetically talks to her *'sweet mother'* (p. 158, l. 19) – an obscene word to him – and ridicules the social values of the time.

Points to remember

- Shakespeare's thoughts and words serve as a contrast to the superficiality of the World State.
- His words also serve as a warning against using other people's words to describe one's own reality.

Henry Ford and Mass Production

In the predominantly agricultural societies of the past, the life of the vast majority of the population had been very simple, if not miserable, with luxuries being reserved for a tiny elite. The Industrial Revolution which began in England in the 18th century brought about a significant change in the living standards of the masses. During the 19th and early 20th centuries methods of production continually improved, with America leading the way in the 20th century. During his journey to the USA in 1925/26, Huxley was very impressed by the technological progress he witnessed.

Henry Ford and his assembly line

Huxley chose Henry Ford as the symbolic demi-god of mass culture and the founder of a new era for two reasons: his use of the assembly line signals the beginning of mass production, and his product – the mass-produced automobile – stands for individual mobility and almost unlimited opportunities. The assembly line allowed Ford to keep costs down so that his cars were affordable for the average citizen, instead of being luxury items reserved for the upper classes. The Ford Model T sold more than 15,000,000 units, becoming the greatest automobile success story of the time; it was a record that stood for almost half a century.

Moreover, Ford's name rhymes with 'Lord', a religious appellation for God, which allowed Huxley to use a lot of puns throughout the novel based on the name (*'Oh, Ford'*, p.27, l.25). The rhyme allowed the author to transfer expressions from the Christian religion to the world of the novel. The same applies for Ford's Model T. In the World State, the letter T not only replaces the Christian sign of the cross, but it has also taken over place names in London, like Charing T instead of Charing Cross.

The following technological milestones may have influenced Huxley when he was writing *Brave New World*:

- Helicopters: Early models were developed in the 1920s, the first viable helicopter was built in 1936 in Germany.
- Movies: Silent movies were shown from the beginning of the 20th century. In the 1920s the technological development made it possible to add sounds, these films were called 'talkies' (for 'talking pictures', hence the term 'feely' in the novel).
- TV: The first experimental transmission took place in London in 1925, colour TV followed in 1928.
- Contraception: By 1930 scientists had discovered that high doses of certain hormones could inhibit ovulation, although it was only in the 1960s that the 'the Pill' became available.

Points to remember

- Huxley saw Ford as being the industrialist who first introduced the world to the potential of new forms of production.
- Huxley feared that mass production would dehumanize us, and that we might ourselves become products of mass production.

Conditioning

Classical Conditioning is a theory of learning. It is based on the assumption that human beings and animals can learn certain patterns of behaviour by connecting a stimulus with a certain response.

The famous experiment that laid down the foundation of classical conditioning was carried out by the Russian scientist Ivan Petrovich Pavlov (1849–1936) on dogs (Pavlov's dogs). When dogs are hungry they begin to produce saliva (unconditioned response) as soon as they notice something to eat (unconditioned stimulus). In his experiment Pavlov used certain types of stimuli (e.g. bells) whenever he called the dogs to their food. He discovered that after repeating the stimulus together with the food several times, the dogs started salivating when the stimulus was present, even if there was no food present. Thus, the originally neutral stimulus triggered the same response (conditioned response) that food had evoked before. Pavlov called the combination of the stimulus and the reaction of the dogs a conditioned reflex.

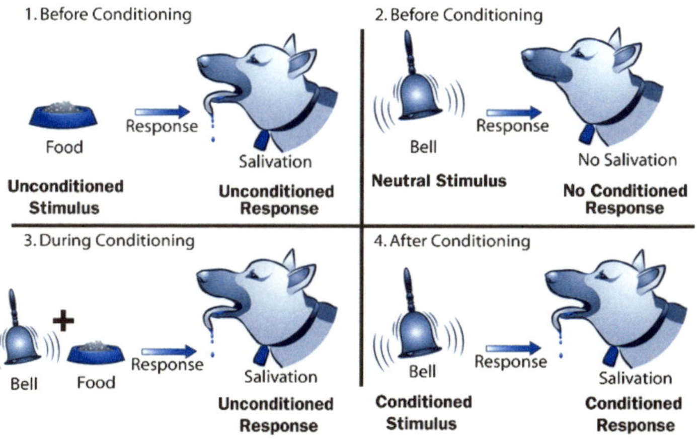

However, if the dog learns after several repetitions that the bell does not mean food, the reflex is lost again (extinction).

For his discoveries about the digestive system Pavlov was awarded the Nobel Prize in Medicine in 1904, but the theory of conditioning turned out to be much more influential in science as well as in popular culture. The phrase 'Pavlov's dogs' became famous and was used to describe someone who reacts to a situation almost automatically, instead of using critical thinking. In *Brave New World* the Russian scientist is alluded to in the '*Neo-Pavlovian Conditioning Rooms*' (p. 19, l. 4), an essential part of the 'Hatchery and Conditioning Centre'.

The American psychologist John B. Watson (1878–1958) transferred Pavlov's findings to human beings and developed the theory of behaviourism. In his famous Little Albert experiment in 1920, which would be regarded as unethical today, he instilled a conditioned reflex in a nine-month-old baby. Albert was presented with a white rat (and other animals and objects). Like most children he showed curiosity and started playing with the animal. Then Watson produced a loud and unpleasant sound (unconditioned stimulus) which scared the baby and made it cry. After several repetitions of this procedure, Little Albert immediately started to cry and show symptoms of fear whenever he saw the rat. So Albert had associated the loud noise with the rat, thereby making an originally neutral stimulus a conditioned one. His fearful reaction to the noise (unconditioned, because all children react with fear to loud and unpleasant sounds) had been transferred to the rat as a conditioned response.

After being conditioned in such a way, people experience fear when presented with any stimulus that has similarities to the original conditioned response. So Little Albert, for instance, was afterwards afraid of rabbits and other hairy things. Principally, there are two ways of making human beings lose their conditioned fear again: habituating them by constantly exposing them to the stimulus they fear, so that the stimulus loses its threat; or re-conditioning by associating positive feelings with what caused uneasiness before. Both methods are still used in psycho-therapy, but do not always work.

The theory of conditioning, and particularly the Little Albert experiment, must have impressed Huxley deeply, as the conditioning depicted in the *Brave New World* is modelled on it. Having perfected conditioning, and by constantly repeating that learning process, the World State determines the lifelong likes and dislikes of its citizens. The process is demonstrated to the students who watch infants being conditioned against books and flowers with the help of extremely unpleasant noises and electric shocks. That procedure will be repeated

200 times to ensure that they '*will be safe from books and botany all their lives*' (p. 21, l. 23), which will shift their interests to things that require equipment and keep the production process going. Another example of conditioning is the death-conditioning in Park Lane Hospital: here, a group of eight-year-old children is taught to connect pain and death with something positive, in this case chocolate éclairs.

It should be remembered that Huxley was satirizing the views of behaviourists like Watson, who believed that the human being could be reduced to a simple stimulus-response procedure.

Points to remember

- Conditioning is a process that teaches people to react in a certain way to certain stimuli.
- Conditioning is the basis of education in the World State.

Glossary of Terms Used in the Novel

Bokanovsky's Process (Bokanovskification): method of treating an egg with X-rays and alcohol to produce up to 96 identical twins. (pp. 7ff.)

Bottling: process of putting artificially-created embryos into bottles on an assembly line to facilitate treatment. (pp. 10ff.)

Caste: social group to which a person belongs. The castes are named after the Greek letters Alpha, Beta, Gamma, Delta, and Epsilon. These castes are differentiated by intelligence (the result of adding alcohol in different amounts to the embryos), their function in society, and their clothing. However, conditioning (➔) makes each person satisfied with their particular caste so that no conflicts arise from the differences.

Community Sing: pseudo-religious celebration for large groups of people. (p. 68)

Conditioning: method of teaching behaviour patterns with the help of punishments (e.g. electric shocks) and rewards (e.g. chocolate éclairs). Conditioning is complemented by hypnopaedia (➔). (pp. 16ff.)

Decanting: equivalent of natural birth (to decant sth. means to pour sth. out of a bottle). (p. 125)

Ectogenesis: fertilization of the human egg and ripening of the embryo outside the female womb. (p. 42)

Emotional engineering: state propaganda (in the forms of movies, slogans, etc.) that keeps the population in harmony with the state. (p. 57)

Feely: type of cinematic film, in which the audience also feels the action (for "feeling pictures", adapted from "talky", i.e. "talking pictures"). (pp. 142ff.)

Ford, Henry (1863–1947): American car producer and the idol of the World State (which refers to him as 'Our Ford')

Freemartin: woman who was sterilized as an embryo, as eggs are not needed from every woman. (p. 14)

Games: leisure activities such as Centrifugal Bumble-Puppy, Electro-magnetic Golf, Escalator Squash, Obstacle Golf, Riemann-Surface Tennis, whose purpose is to entertain the masses with activities that keep production going due to the need for equipment.

Hatchery: the building in which people are created, formed and born. (p. 5)

Hypnopaedia: sleep-teaching of moral values by endless repetitions during childhood. As a part of life-long conditioning (➔), hypnopaedia is one of the basic control techniques of the World State. (pp. 24ff.)

Hypnopaedic slogans: phrases that are played to the citizens in their sleep as they grow up. Here is a list of some of the slogans:

Never put off till tomorrow the fun you can have today.
When the individual feels, the community reels.
Everyone belongs to everyone else.
Ending is better than mending.
The more stitches the less riches.
Cleanliness is next to fondliness.
Civilization is sterilization.
Everybody's happy now.
A doctor a day keeps the jim-jams away.

Relating to *soma* (➔):

A gramme in time saves nine.
Was and will make me ill. I take a gramme and only am.
One cubic centimeter cures ten gloomy sentiments.
A gramme is always better than a damn.

Malthusian Drill: training to prevent unsterilized women from becoming pregnant; named after the British economist Thomas Malthus (1766–1834) who warned of the fatal effects of overpopulation. (p. 67)

Nine Years' War: Turning point in history in A.F. 141 when a dirty war with anthrax bombs and infected water supplies (a reference to World War I) caused countless casualties and the great Economical Collapse (suggesting the World Economic Crisis of 1929). As the only alternative to complete destruction, the World State was established. (pp. 43ff., 196)

Podsnap's Technique: Process of accelerating the ripening of eggs so that the number of offspring from one ovary can be increased considerably. (p. 9)

Predestination: the formation of the individual embryo for its future in society. (pp. 11ff.)

Pregnancy substitute: treatment that stabilizes women emotionally so that they can enjoy a promiscuous sex-life. (p. 35)

Reservation: area in New Mexico where Indians still live in traditional systems. It is surrounded by an electric fence that prevents escape, while access from outside requires a special permit. In the novel the Reservation serves as a contrast to the modern world. (pp. 92ff.)

Solidarity Service: pseudo-religious ceremony culminating in the ecstatic unification of the 'orgy-porgy'; a parody of Christian services. (pp. 67ff.)

***Soma*:** euphoric drug without side-effects that is taken whenever people want to cheer themselves up (*'All the advantages of Christianity and alcohol; none of their defects'*; p. 48, l. 3). The consumption of *soma* guarantees the emotional stability of the individual and hence of society.

T: the equivalent of the Christian cross, named after Henry Ford's popular car the T-Model. (p. 24)

Violent Passion Surrogate (VPS): treatment in which the body is regularly flooded with adrenalin, replacing strong emotions like rage and fear without their unpleasant consequences. (p. 206)

World State: this is the only name (apart from 'civilized place') which is used for the society depicted in *Brave New World*.

Glossary of Literary Terms

character, flat: a character that has a limited number of traits or represents a single quality, and does not develop in the course of the action.

character, round: a character that usually changes in the course of the action, has more than just a single trait and tends to be life-like.

dystopian literature: a fictional text dealing with a perfectly organized and usually futuristic society, in which human freedom is severely limited or in which some other sort of unpleasant feature characterizes the otherwise perfect society.

extrapolation: the technique of working out and describing how the future will look on the basis of already known facts. Extrapolation is the foundation of utopian and dystopian literature, as the author exaggerates certain aspects of his or her own society to create a new one.

flashback: a scene or an event that took place before the action in a novel or story.

figurative meaning: a word has a literal meaning (which takes a word at its face value) and a figurative meaning, which refers to another meaning beyond that of its immediate and basic message. The "moon", for example, in its literal sense is the planet, but it may have many more implications like "the future", "imagination", "love" or "madness". Figurative language includes images, metaphors and symbols.

metaphor: a figure of speech describing one thing in terms of another, so as to suggest some common quality shared by the two.

motif: a theme, an image or incident that is repeated significantly within a single work. It is sometimes also referred to as a *leitmotif*.

narrator: the voice of the person who tells the story in a novel and is part of the fictional world created by the author.

symbol: an object, word or phrase signifying something concrete that stands not only for itself but for an abstract idea.

third-person narrator: a third-person narrator is not a character in the story. He refers to the characters as 'he', 'she' or 'they'.

utopian literature: a fictional text dealing with an ideal society. Utopias, like dystopias, usually aim at telling the reader something about the world in which they live.

Coping with Exam Papers

Generally, tasks on texts, whether they are fictional or non-fictional, fall into three categories: 1) **comprehension**, 2) **analysis** and 3) writing a **composition** or a **personal comment**.

1. Comprehension

All comprehension tasks aim at finding out whether you have **understood** the novel. Usually you are given an extract and are asked to locate it within the framework of the whole novel. You must select the relevant events which lead up to the extract and which take place afterwards. When answering comprehension questions you should refrain from stating your own opinion, unless expressly asked to do so.

2. Analysis

Analysis tasks go beyond a simple understanding of the text. You may be asked to deal with the whole novel or to deal with the selected extract in detail. Analysis questions often concern language and imagery, characters, or the way the plot is structured. Here again, you should avoid giving your own opinion. Be careful not to retell the story: you really need to analyse what is happening on a more abstract level, e.g. don't just say what a character does, but explain why he or she does it, or find an adjective to describe the character, etc.

3. Evaluation

This area covers a wide range of different tasks. Indeed you may be offered a choice of two tasks.

You may be asked to write a **composition** or a **comment**, which often require you to show that you have understood what the intention of the story is. Tasks often deal with a general interpretation of the novel so make sure your ideas are plausible and well argued. This means that your ideas have to be in line with the novel and that you must always be able to prove what you say by referring to the stories. Never just make a supposition and leave it at that.

You may be asked to write a 'personal comment', which means you are obliged to give your own opinion, so make sure you base it on informed judgement, for which you need a thorough knowledge not just of the novel but also of the way it is constructed, so avoid making statements which you cannot prove.

Often you will be given the choice of doing a 'creative task'. Although at first this may seem easy, you should only choose to do a creative task if you have practised enough beforehand and your teacher seems happy with your work in this area. Creative tasks can involve:

- a change of perspective (i.e. recounting events or situations from the point of view of another character);
- reflection on other characters or events: this can often be in the form of a diary entry;
- filling in the gaps: here you might be asked to fill in what the reader does not learn directly from the text. This can often be in the form of a letter, an extra scene or an additional piece of dialogue.

Whatever kind of creative tasks are set, you must remember to stay within the context of the novel. This means that you must not simply fantasize but look, for example, at the way a certain character behaves.

Operative Words

Regardless of which category of tasks you are dealing with, it is extremely important to read the task carefully and look for the operative words, which tell you exactly what is required of you. Here is a list of common operative words, in alphabetical order. (They are not necessarily confined to comprehension, analysis or composition)

Analyse ...: an analysis is a detailed examination of, for example, an important topic, the narrative technique, or one or more of the characters, so you must deal carefully with all the relevant aspects.

Assess ...: here, you must consider in a balanced way the points for and against something.

Comment on ...: here you are allowed to give your personal opinion on, say, narrative technique or the way characters behave, but you must always give evidence from the novel to support it.

Compare ...: you must highlight similarities and differences, most frequently between characters and events. A similar kind of task is:

Contrast ...: here, however, you should concentrate on the differences.

Describe ...: in this kind of task you must show what something (e.g. setting) or somebody (one or more of the characters) is like by giving a detailed account. Be careful not to forget any relevant details and choose examples from the text to illustrate the points you have made.

Discuss …: if you are asked to discuss a particular aspect of the novel (e.g. its narrative technique or the characters and how they interact), you should examine the issue from all sides before you state your personal opinion.

Evaluate …: here, you must form an opinion after carefully considering and presenting the advantages and disadvantages of a particular situation or course of action.

Examine …: this is another way of asking you to **analyse** something.

Explain …: this kind of task involves giving reasons for the action, characters' motives or how the specific use of certain techniques like the use of imagery or modes of description produce a certain effect.

Characterize/Describe somebody's character …: here you should describe the specific features of, most often, one or more characters, by looking at how they are presented and the way they speak.

Illustrate …: here, you have to make something clear by choosing relevant examples. Read the task carefully to find out whether you have to concentrate on the given passage or whether you may, or have to, refer to the whole novel.

Interpret …: here you should deal with both form and content and how they work together to create meaning.

Justify …: here you must argue why something should be done or some decision taken or why some conclusion was made.

Outline …: an outline is a general account of something. In other words in your outline you can re-tell the major events of a story, or give a brief description of a character, which includes only the very relevant elements only and omits all details.

Point out …: here, you must find and explain certain aspects of the text.

Present …: here, you are expected to write something down in your words.

State …: here, you are expected to specify clearly whatever is required. You may be required to state the main features of or development of something.

Summarize …: a summary is more precise than an outline. When writing a summary you should select the key points and ideas etc. and structure them. As in an outline you should not go into detail or give examples. You might, for example, be asked to summarize a dialogue or argument, or the events of the whole novel or an extract.

General points to remember – or how to impress the examiner:

- You are not writing for yourself, but you are addressing the examiner(s) who will mark your work. Examiners are not mind-readers, so you must express yourself as clearly as possible.
- Always collect and organize your ideas before you start writing. In this way the examiner will be able to follow you more easily.
- When writing a composition or a personal comment, remember three simple steps: say what you are going to say – say it – sum up what you have said. Doing this will make your text more convincing.
- When you are dealing with literature you should always use the simple present tense when discussing characters and action.
- Structure your work by using '**connectives**' to link your ideas, so that the examiner can follow the presentation of your arguments. Otherwise he or she gets the impression that you are 'rambling'. You should be able to find a list of connectives in your coursebook.
- Likewise, avoid all forms of repetition, unless you want to return to a point you made earlier on. In this case you should use expressions like 'as I have already pointed out …'
- You can always impress the examiner by using suitable quotes, but they should only be used to **underline** a point you have already made or are going to make, and not instead of making a point – otherwise the examiner will think you are simply copying from the text or that you are unable to express yourself correctly. Always put your quotations in inverted commas. If you are allowed to use the book, you should also refer to the page and line of the quote.
- Usually the test paper will tell you how many words you have to write for each section of the test. If you have time after re-reading and checking your paper for coherence, mistakes, etc., try and count your words, as you may have marks deducted for writing too little or too much.

Written Test

Test

Aldous Huxley, *Brave New World*
Excerpt from Chapter 16 (p. 191, l. 12 – p. 193, l. 11)

Tasks

1. **Describe the Cyprus experiment and explain what it reveals.**
2. **Explain the role of work in the World State.**
3. **Where would you prefer to live – in today's society or in the futuristic World State? Write a comment.**

Dealing with the Test

The following are not to be considered model solutions, but hints and ideas to help you write your own answer.

1

In this assignment you are first asked to summarize in your own words a specific section of the text.

- All the inhabitants of Cyprus were removed and replaced with Alphas.
- The Alphas had to take on every job necessary to keep society functioning, regardless of their talents.
- However, the Alphas started competing for the better jobs, so the agricultural and industrial jobs were not done. Society became lawless.
- Within six years a civil war had broken out, and the inhabitants asked the World State to take control again.

In the second part of the task you are asked to analyse why the situation developed as it did, and describe the lessons that can be learned from it.

- Every society needs a variety of people to make it function. Each society consists of different classes (based on talent, intelligence, upbringing etc.) who fulfill different functions.
- Talented people are not satisfied with doing menial work.
- Competition becomes intense when the majority of jobs are menial with only a minority of jobs involving responsibility.
- Society can never be truly equal.

2

Once again analysis is required here. Information is provided in this section about the role of work. First of all, gather the information:

- Alphas would go mad if they did Epsilon work.
- Epsilons are happy doing Epsilon work.
- Work is a form of occupation.
- Too much leisure can lead to boredom.

Then reach some conclusions about the role of work in the World State:

- People do the work for which they are best suited.
- People with limited intelligence enjoy doing the work that suits them.
- Work is a way of keeping people happy, even if it appears that the work is not always necessary.

3

To answer this question you will have to list various features of the World State that you consider either positive or negative about their society. These might be:

- Happiness.
- The absence of illness, hunger, war, etc.
- The method of producing and conditioning human beings.
- The absence of families.
- Sexual promiscuity.
- The use of *soma.*
- The rigid caste system.
- The feelies and other entertainment.
- Etc.

Then you must decide which, in your opinion, are positive and which are negative. It is your personal opinion, so you must be able to support your point of view, even if others might disagree.